Black Apples of Gower

STONE-FOOTING
IN MEMORY FIELDS

IAIN SINCLAIR

A LITTLE TOLLER **MONOGRAPH**

First published by Little Toller Books in 2015

Little Toller Books, Lower Dairy, Toller Fratrum, Dorset DT2 OEL

Words © Iain Sinclair 2016

Jacket and all internal images by Ceri Richards © The Estate of Ceri Richards:

Frontispiece (Pastel sketch of Gower cliffs, heron and horse tipped-in to a copy of *Fidelities* by Vernon Watkins), **pages 89** (above: *The Author's Prologue*, below: *The force that through the green fuse*), **page 91** ('I dreamed my genesis' from *Drawings to Poems by Dylan Thomas*), **page 94** (*Do not go gentle into that good night*), **page 99** (*Homage to Dylan Thomas*), **page 106** (Ink and pastel sketch of heron with fish, june 1971, tipped-in to a copy of *The Poems* by Dylan Thomas), **page 108** (*Black Apple of Gower, Afal du Brogwyr*), **page 117** (*La Cathédrale engloutie: profondément calme*), **page 119** (*La Cathédrale engloutie: profondément calme*) **and page 121** (*La Cathédrale engloutie: Sunrise I*)

All Ceri Richards work has been reproduced from Mel Gooding's *Ceri Richards* (2002) by courtesy of Jill Hollis at Cameron & Hollis, except the Frontispiece and page 106, which were courtesy of Rhiannon and Mel Gooding.

All additional images Iain Sinclair 2015 except:

page 18 Dylan Thomas © The John Deakin Archive / Getty Images **pages 69, 81 and 153** Gower sketches by Brian Catling © Brian Catling and Iain Sinclair **page 73** Postcard © Laurence 'Renchi' Bicknell and Iain Sinclair **pages 45, 53 and 85** © Gwen Watkins and the Estate of Vernon Watkins **page 176** *Totes Meer* by Paul Nash © Tate **page 178** *St Nicholas of Bari Rebuking the Storm* by Bicci di Lorenzo © Ashmolean Museum

Typeset in Garamond and Perpetua by Little Toller

Printed by GraphyCems, Navarra

All papers used by Little Toller Books are natural, recyclable products made from wood grown in sustainable, well-managed forests

A catalogue record for this book is available from the British Library

ISBN 978-1-908213-45-7

01

For Anna and William

'If one string of a bone crosses another properly, an area of brightness or intensity is created, so that a skeleton, because it was hidden, appears to have been exposed, almost inadvertently.'
RICHARD TUTTLE

'The Welshman's voice was fractured limestone.'
MICHAEL MOORCOCK

'I say my farewells and return to my cave, where I sleep a peaceful and dreamless journey.'
BRIAN CATLING

CONTENTS

HORTON

Out of the deserted car park, through a lightly grassed cleft in the dunes and on to the beach: that sudden heart-stopping rush of light and space; the scoop of shore, a dazzling meniscus of smooth, firm sand under marine heaven. A beach that is always *the* beach. As wide and inviting and warm underfoot as it was back then, in the bathysphere of dream where it remains first sight every time.

My responses, on this bright September day in 2014, are predictable, obedient to the genre of the Celtic return: the crumpled boyo skulking back to the shop-soiled plot of innocence, after years venturing in murky elsewheres and making them so familiar that the inherited racial compass is completely wrecked. The shooting script of the Gower shoreline, in late afternoon, approaching the golden hour, feels pre-written, but not quite redundant. I'm eager to blow the dust from the top of a slim volume of autobiography left on the shelf for decades. Sonar echoes are muffled, but Dylan Thomas-infected prospects of the sea are overwhelming. I call up the famous photograph of the poet in the BBC studio, leaning on an elbow, puffy-faced; a turtle-necked bohemian confronted by a microphone as threatening as Nuremburg.

'The afternoon was dying; lazily, namelessly drifting westward.' Memory-spill tame as a wet bank holiday. 'A wince and whinny of bathers dancing into deceptive water.' The past is a sandy tablet for sketching and charming and not paying bills for the guilt of prolonged absence. We are looking for private islands, coming in half asleep on some rattling bus, and finding no good reason to leave. Language pirates, raiders, gatherers up of other men's rescued trifles.

If I were to recommend the walk that gave the sharpest jolt to my imagination, it would not be in London. Those Thames bank expeditions were prose: laboured documentation back-channelling a selective mythology. Ejaculations of hopelessness. The walks that truly haunt, and hurt, are the ones that walk you. They anticipate future projects known before the first fatal step is risked. So the day's expedition – and it is always a day – is the recognition of the distance to be experienced but never understood or captured or made safe.

Horton was a self-contained village on the edge of

amnesia, situated at around the mid-point of Port Eynon Bay, on the southern ledge of the Gower Peninsula. My family had a caravan with a hillside perch in a farmer's field, shared with five or six others, overlooking the spread of shore. Sunset was an event worth stepping outside, cup in hand, to witness. This was where, in my teenage years, I spent my holidays, in remission from the strictures of boarding school, the regulated existence within a hometown where everyone knew everyone else's business. The blessing of this 2014 return was in being anonymous in a new place, open to all its undiscovered magic. In this village, in the caravan days, it was a privileged form of camping: milk and water to be collected from the farmyard, hissing gas lamps to be managed. Soft glow over the foldaway table of paperbacks and board games. The lost-life pictures are still there, but they are crisped and sered like Polaroids that have faded, for lack of interest, in a locked drawer. Physical sensations, odours especially – puddled, stone-floored byre, chemical toilet, melting tarmac, clover dunes, bubbling chip vats – invoke home-movie episodes as they might or might not have happened. But the *real*, the authentic grip of locality, is in the rocks. The arms of the bay. The muscular headlands of Oxwich Point and Port Eynon Point. And the straggle of cliff paths between them. And that vision, when the tide retreats, of Carboniferous wave-cut limestone pavements: fractured, monochromatic. An alien planet revealed, submerged, revealed again. A lunar colony with no traces of past or future inhabitants. A terrain that is, simultaneously, before and after any whisper of civilisation.

*

We travelled from London, making the unfamiliar drive along the northern rim of Gower, down the Loughor Estuary, after coming off the torrent of the M4 at Junction 47, on the approach to Gorseinon – where I'd been sent, aged seven, to stay with relatives, as a trial run for boarding school. What I remember is nothing to do with the strange bedroom I was allocated or my well-disposed temporary guardians, but the novelty of that blue-grey road, promising so much, running to who knows where, beside tidy houses and the occasional mysterious shop. Setting out to walk a few hundred yards of highway somewhere beyond the hungry sprawl of Swansea was a harbinger for much that followed. I relished it more than the compulsory Sunday nature-trail tramps through the sand dunes that formed part of the routine of the prep school in Nottage, a village on the outskirts of Porthcawl. My preferred nature studies were abandoned tin works, landfill quarries, feeder pipes, slag heaps, rust-red streams, overgrown railway embankments, and not the approved catalogue of rabbits, hawks, herons, butterflies, beetles, spiders, mallow, rock spurrey and gentian.

Gower has a proud otherness. It claims to be a severed English community, in exile from the 'true' side of the Bristol Channel; close-bred, tight with its cash, upgraded from the era of fishers and wreckers to the condescending exploitation of seasonal visitors. Now, as we discovered, after completing our walk and moving on to Swansea by the old coast road, through Penmaen and Parkmill, the principal source of income for the area was not tourism but parking fees. Traffic was unremitting. The celebrated beaches at Oxwich and Three Cliffs were advertised, but no drivers could slow down long enough to read the road signs. Before you could so much as unfold a map, you needed a parking permit. Even roadside pubs charge you for the privilege of walking across gravel to inspect the menu. Convenience stores make most of their profit from migrants trapped in their vehicles, too frightened to buy an ice cream, or essential supplies for the caravan, without losing a ticketed slot. This was the route we used to cycle, as we relished coming to terms with the Peninsula's assertion of difference, those narrow lanes and high hedges.

Arriving by a new route – we were staying in a country-house hotel, near Reynoldston – offered easy access to the ritual of acclimatisation first experienced in the late 1950s and early '60s. Sheep paddling on salt marshes. Cockle harvesters at Penclawdd. Solitary stands of evergreens. Novelties taking us away from our London lives. I knew that the ashes of Ernest Jones, the psychoanalyst and approved biographer of Freud, were buried at St Cadoc's church in Cheriton. But that was for another day. Jones, a man of wide interests, publishing on ice-skating and chess, was the person responsible for having Gower declared an 'Area of Outstanding Natural Beauty'. He helped to bring Freud out of Austria to London.

Slowing down, stopping to inspect the coastal view or check on another closed pub, we were decontaminated after the centrifugal thrust of the motorway. The novelist Rudolph Wurlitzer has a nice title for the liminal terrain in which we found ourselves as afternoon light shifted gracefully through the f-stops: *The Drop Edge of Yonder.* Without closing my eyes, I had the feeling of returning to the wrong body, or the wrong place, that comes after the short, sweet blackout of a deep afternoon siesta. Wurlitzer quotes the Lankavatara Sutra: 'Things are not as they appear. Nor are they otherwise.' He speaks of a recurrent dream: 'A long endless fall through an empty sky towards a storm-tossed sea.' The figures standing over him, when he returns to consciousness, are hungry ghosts clutching corpse candles.

Our approach to the hotel is not like that. There are no humans on the road and few markers beyond suspect grey stones that resolve into affronted sheep. We are the only ghosts, hungry for stories to infiltrate, confirmation of a past that never happened. If we do not find a holloway path into a landscape sanctioned by some previous authority, we are left in the limbo of creatures without tribe or history.

Our ivy-draped refuge, with its legend of recovery from ruin, its tactfully restored bedrooms with views across shaved lawns where television interviews are now being staged, insulates guests in a subtle cocoon, as if nothing they touched should be hard enough to bruise. The selling point is a temporary suspension of reality, straight back to an Edwardian summer, with weekend guests paying for hospitality. The only residue of the known is that film of the motorway: steel mills, blast furnace, smoke columns, crematorium. Abbey, sculpture park, storage units. Tight-packed terraces, pegged to a blue hump of hillside, masking the former mining town where I grew up.

I wanted to get straight out to the beach, to fix my bearings before, early tomorrow, we started the walk that held all the answers: Port Eynon Point to Worm's Head and Rhossili.

Those few miles, scrambling, descending, poking into caves, were a memory map, as much invented as catalogued. I did it the first time when I was about sixteen and holidaying with two friends in the Horton caravan. Nothing quite fitted with the impressions I dredged up, fifty-six years later. The village was so white, so brightly painted. Some of the old synapses still fired, other pieces of the cortical jigsaw had been forced into the wrong slots. I remembered walking slowly down a winding road from farm to sea. Driving, talking to my wife, everything happened too fast.

The mechanics of opening the car door, finding a towel, getting the right coins into the slot for our parking fee, helped my orientation. The quiddity of Horton is not as pronounced as that of Laugharne on the River Taf or New Quay in Cardigan. The inhabitants are not as eccentric or potentially perverse. Dylan Thomas could not have inflicted his postmortem dreams on this sequestered stretch of the Gower. The rocks are too old, too active. *Under Milk Wood* is an estuary piece; tidal, convulsive, squeezed out of money-terror, alcohol, sleeping pills, cortisone, performance sweat, last days, sirens, ambulances. Pre-posthumous. The play belongs in the fond sleep of the burying ground where Dylan was photographed, in rehearsal for mortality, by John Deakin. It is not the slow layering, heaping up and scratching away at reference and cross-reference, of *Finnegans Wake*. Which does not begin at the beginning, but way out beyond the end, in transit: *riverrun, swerve of shore*. Graves open for Dylan, as for Stanley Spencer, on the local; known individuals who become types and archetypes, ready and willing to give him welcome. He sleepwalks through a lack of structure.

He names names, and he names places, for the sound and sentiment of it: Mumbles, Dowlais, Maesgwyn. *White field.* And the rivers: Ely, Gwili, Ogwr, Nedd. There is no spiral geometry, no definition, just mood and momentum; where Joyce articulates every bitter nuance, shoreline as architecture. The two headlands: 'Save me from those therrble prongs!' They say that at the end of the last Ice Age – which begins to feel like yesterday – the man who left his bones in one of the

Gower caves could have walked to Ireland. Carrying, tattooed on his back, the prophecy of *The Mabinogion*, for presentation to James Joyce, Samuel Beckett and Flann O'Brien.

And so driving the last few miles from Scurlage, then the country lane, I'm imposing half-remembered sets on evidence that refuses to support my notion of what the fields should hold. There are many more caravans now. Orchards are planted with rows of tin. Camps and settlements for recreationalists, not seasonal labourers. Unmanaged thickets were cropped back. I thought of a Dylan Thomas story from 1936. 'He had dreamed that a hundred orchards on the road to the sea village had broken into flame; and all the windless afternoon tongues of fire shot through the blossom . . . He was an apple-farmer in a dream that ended as it began.'

There was one other swimmer, a woman, sturdy in her black costume, probably a local following a well established regime. Cousin to the porpoises. The sea knew her. She'd live forever. I'm sure she was here, same age, same size, same confidence, hair matted with salt, when I was fifteen.

The first thing that struck me was the width of the bay. I did most of my swimming, before coffee, before work, in St Leonards on the south coast, East Sussex. Peppery red shingle. Corrugated meadows of steelgrey water leaking into an illuminated arc of sky. The beach was an exhibition, units divided by wooden fence-post groynes. Against one of which, on Christmas Day, a woman taking a walk was dashed by a wave, and killed. The stretch in front of the 1930s concrete boat-building in which we had a flat, favoured by hardy wild-water men, was curated like a performance-art video between two piers: the torched skeleton to the east, jutting out from White Rock, and the spectral afterimage of the demolished and removed St Leonards pier to the west. This strip of shore, tracked by a broad esplanade with, beneath it, a series of curved recesses sometimes occupied by affable knots of drinkers, was always busy. Couples holding each other upright against the wind. Stopped visitors mesmerised by the spectacle of relentless waves, like the wash of gigantic, unseen container ships. Cyclists. Solitaries trudging back to their nests, in ballast, with twin shopping bags. So that the simple act of taking a morning dip became one detail in a vivid social document, the theatre of place. On shore, folk leaned on the railings to watch. Swimmers kept an eye on their towels and bags, wary of skittering dogs and metal-detecting scavengers. One man, well fleshed, plodded down the steps, across the sharp stones, and out towards the Hastings pier, forcing himself through the swell with urgent, choppy strokes. He came at all seasons, barefoot, trunks, nothing else. Then back, dripping, through the traffic, up the steps again, away. He was tired of having his shoes, shirts and towels stolen. He stripped the exercise to its bare essentials. Elective hypothermia. Brain rush. Engagement.

I associated my swims at St Leonards with cinema. The vanished pier was referenced by a metal plaque with relief lettering, to be fingered by those of uncertain sight. The legend reported that this was where the first moving pictures in the town were shown on November 7, 1896. You could imagine shadows of trains and trams and captured lightning projected above the waves. And that tradition continued, to the point where the filmmaker Andrew Kötting, along with brothers, cousins, actors and in-laws, swam in a relay to France. I accompanied them, with sick bucket, blankets and hot sweet tea. The ship-of-fools expedition confirmed my impression of the English Channel as a motorway, animated by twin streams of heavy traffic, towering red hulks marking the horizon on clear evenings.

Horton was nothing like that. I paddled out in the wake of the woman in the black costume. I felt the two arms of the protected bay, but the pull of the tide was not fierce. Down here, I wasn't caught up in a series of arbitrary divisions like a field system after the Agricultural Enclosure Acts. On some mornings in St Leonards I had to work hard, lazy breaststroking wouldn't do it, to stay where I was and not to drift two or three groynes east towards the pier. In the Gower, the water wasn't cloudy with sediment or scummed over with malodorous brown life forms, a foaming plankton fringe. This late-afternoon dip washed away the road miles, the distance from London, and floated me out of the time fix. My gentle wallow became an initiation reconnecting me with necessary specifics of place before the next day's coastal walk.

Swimming was about not belonging, confirming the years I had travelled away from those Horton holidays. It was a potent reminder of justified criticism I faced, in Wales, for trying to re-establish a tentative connection with my homeland in a novel of the borders, *Landor's Tower*. I had forfeited all those advantages of birth, walked away from a bankable heritage. Swimming made the not-belonging absolute. And liberating. As I took the first few strokes, drifted, struck out, drifted again, I forged a link, however unreliable, with previous swims – believing, at the same time, that all swims are previous; linear time doesn't operate in the ocean. There was the heat of youthful plunges, groups of us, coming through the dunes, days on the beach. There are black-and-white photographs, prints of impersonators we have to take on trust. And even earlier times, when the Bristol Channel was always cold; coming down, a few years after the war, from the Porthcawl prep school, through a caravan park, for a shivering compulsory plunge. And the way that a beach, under constant revision of wind and tide, stays the same. With only the word – *beach* – altering its meaning with the decades. As we live further from the reality, walled in by miles of city streets, ribbon-developed suburbs. Swimming offered the required medium in which to contemplate the narrative of the rocks.

The woman in black walked up the beach, wet footprints in the sand. Beyond her, against the line of the dunes, someone looking very much like my wife, like Anna, was dozing. It was too far away to be sure. In turning, thirty yards out, to face the shoreline, all the elements of the past I was struggling to identify became suddenly clear: the point where our caravan had parked, the hill and thicket of trees below it, the cliff path running west towards Oxwich Point. These were facts, certain distances to be walked. Horton was true again. And not, as it had been for many years, a dream promontory. Or scaffold of unanchored fantasy. A quotation with no attributed source. Dream walks were always in twilight, when inner and outer forms of illumination mingle. I was quite alone now, disembodied;

not son or husband or father. Walking on soft ground among soft shapes, trusting to blind instinct, sinking back into the perpetual sleep of place.

Around the time I stopped coming to Horton, and after the caravan was sold, I visited Vernon Watkins in his bungalow at Pennard. He was the poet of Gower, of the stones, waves, white blossom. Working as a bank clerk in Swansea, and commuting every day by bus, the moment of freedom on his return, when he scampered goat-footed down to the sea, was the release of his hidden self, the one that remained here. Poetry was recognition. Poetry was listening. Fine tuning the cadences of the ear. 'It is fitting to fling off clothing,' Watkins wrote. 'To enter the sea with plunge of sunwreaths white / Broken by limbs that love the waters.' Gower bungalows were clapboard caravans that had taken root on rugs of coarse grass. Pennard was a nest and a retreat. The good place after a short ride out of post-industrial Swansea. They came, the Watkins associates, the Kardomah gang, before and after the war – lunchtime talkers, provincial poets, fish painters, composers – to smoke and josh and caper on headlands, to play croquet and take high tea and lemonade in the house rented by Vernon's father. The family home: *Heatherslade*. There are snapshots of record. And they came to *The Garth*, where Watkins settled with his wife Gwen and their five children. They sunbathed, they walked. 'Inert he lies on the saltgold sand / And sees through his lids the scarlet sky.'

When Dylan Thomas paid a visit – visits were less frequent after he married and established himself as a figure in London – he didn't rush for the water. 'He never seems to have gone in it.' Gwen Watkins quotes the biographer Paul Ferris in her memoir, *Dylan Thomas: Portrait of a Friend.* 'But he did once bathe with Vernon, and in the dark, in October,' Gwen qualifies. 'Sometimes he would throw stones into the water while Vernon swam.'

Caitlin Thomas, on the other hand, like my Horton woman in black, made the sea her element: against the frustrations of married life, that switchback of poverty, bills, scrounging, acceptance of female patronage, and accidents of silly-money windfalls melting like snowflakes in their hot sticky hands. 'Only when bathing or dancing did she throw off the bitterness that by this time pervaded her whole being,' Gwen reported.

If the English Channel struck me as an extension of cinema – burning piers stacked with combustible celluloid, bathing beauty comedies, and contemporary practitioners butting through the swell under a pregnant moon, wearing rubber antlers – then the clarity of the sea at Horton felt like floating through a buoyant archive of memory prints. Opening the eyes, underwater in St Leonards, was a sting of milky cataract vision, like swimming through a drowned building swallowed in sand drifts. Here it felt that it was almost possible to stay down, to learn to breathe with the gills, to read the water as a stratification of photographs, layer after layer of a submerged mythology.

In 2014, late at night, just before Christmas, when I had finished mapping out my scheme for a short account of the walks I had made between Port Eynon Point and Rhossili, and when I had arranged all the photographs of cliffs and caves, blackberries, honeysuckle, sheep, rabbits, into a workable grid, I received, out of the blue, an email from Windsor Jones, next-door neighbour and friend of my childhood in Maesteg. And one of the two teenage boys who came with me on the first walk to Worm's Head. Thinking back, it was shocking to realise that I hadn't seen Windsor since his wedding day, almost half a century ago.

He delivered in rather formal language – 'I regret to

inform you' – bad news. Roger, the third walker on that first expedition, was dead. Throat cancer, cured. Lung cancer, diagnosed and rapidly fatal. While searching for a photograph of Roger from the old days, Windsor discovered another period snapshot, which he now attached.

I'm never adept at printing these things, so the group portrait, from somewhere around 1955, emerged with the heads of the adults sliced off at the neck, until I stuck the two pieces together. In the meditation of the sea, images rapidly dissolve, one into another. Through the Internet, they float on a carousel, flashing and fading, with no more traction than any other promotional shot or cute cameo of family or feline life. The grey capture coughed out by my shuddering printer revealed two adults, four children, all boys, grinning at a stranger, some unknown beach photographer. Cliff and Margaret Jones, the parents, were always hospitable and

welcoming. They included me on family expeditions to the seaside, long drives to Whitesands Bay, near St Davids, with surfboards and cricket bats. And shorter trips to Porthcawl or Southerndown. So here we have, in sandals, varieties of one-size-fits-all rainwear, and short trousers, a stoic troop making a fist of Welsh weather. I have no idea how this freeze-frame accident survived. If that is myself, aged eleven or twelve, no part of that boy-person is now available. The Welsh past is not a foreign country, it's a parallel universe of evidence for the prosecution, supporting dubious fictions of memory. From the large letters – ACH – spilling from the left ear of Cliff Jones, builder, mortician, former butcher and army captain, my guess is that this was Coney Beach, the Porthcawl pleasure-park ripoff of Coney Island. I appear to be toying with coins in the fist, for potential rides and slot machines. Windsor, always a more responsible lad, school cap, ears sticking out, holds his younger brother's hand. To his left is a neighbourhood friend, Clive Lewis. The New Elizabethan age is upon us. The radiant disk of the young queen's portrait shines through the drizzle above the head of a day-tripper in an optimistic white cap. I remember the moment when it was announced in our seaside classroom that the princess's ash-grey, stuttering father had moved into the sleep of history and that the world was now in colour. Starting with the coronation newsreel. And the 'conquest' of Everest.

My marker for this place is not seen. Near the entrance to the fun fair, right by the first ride, the water chute, was a large red apple with a bite taken out of it; a hatch through which those varnished maces on sticks, with their sour green hearts, were inflicted on unsuspecting kids. The monster apple, like the last windfall of an experiment in genetically modified agriculture, belonged to some perverse Disneyfication of the Brothers Grimm. One lick and your tongue sticks to the hard shell around the apple, dark buds hidden inside a glass ball smeared with syrup.

Thinking about the limits of photography, and its

usefulness in reminding us of what remains *outside* the frame, brought to mind another red-green giant from the same apocalyptic orchard. Fixing, so it now seemed, the beginning of the pilgrim route to Gower, our cycle rides, Vernon Watkins on the bus, was the 'Big Apple' of Mumbles, a kiosk originally constructed by a cider company. It dropped from

the sky in the 1930s and has been a landmark ever since. This freakish igloo must have been there on the one occasion when Watkins risked a pub crawl with Dylan Thomas that finished up at The Mermaid in Mumbles. It was Thomas who suffered most when he saw the shadow of the handlebars of the bicycle Vernon was pushing, to hold himself upright, as a set of goat's horns sprouting from his saintly companion's head. 'Dylan became terrified,' Gwen Watkins wrote, 'insisting that he was walking with the devil.'

When we had established email communication, Windsor sent me further photographs, views from walks he took every spring, with his wife, from Rhossili back to their hotel in Oxwich Bay. Seen in digital reproduction, in full colour, the coast path is promoted as valuable heritage. Windsor, although he had lived in England for many years, had a much better relationship than I ever managed with our hometown. He made a detour, after the coast walk, to Llan; to the village church on a hilltop where his parents were buried. He met

Clive for lunch in the pub and he looked after the grave. The last time I was there, I found that the granite stone for my maternal grandparents had snapped away and been left, face down, weathered to the point of erasure. Walking the gentle descent to the church was like a return to the street on which I had lived: the nameplates of my neighbours were now transferred to well-tended graves.

As preparation for tomorrow, a gesture of orientation, I stroll across the beach with Anna. The headland at Port Eynon is contrived from aspects of a broken exhibit that refuses to cohere. One building, the Old Lifeboat House, is still operative as a Youth Hostel. We stayed there on a cycle tour of Wales that took us around the coast to St Davids and on to Strumble Head. Now you can rent a private room for two or four persons of either sex. You can take the whole hostel at the weekend for £300 a night. The massed caravans on the ridge are tactfully screened. The rough stone walls of the former fishing village are as white as a Russian winter.

We investigate the shell of the Salt House: roofless cottages built from locally quarried stone, monochrome blocks with a yellow powdering of lichen; crustose organisms giving painterly lift to a monkish uniformity of grey. The skeletal outline of tumbled walls, doorway slits leading into darkness, contains deep basins used between 1550

and 1650 for the commercial production of salt. Pumped seawater evaporated in metal pans set over a coal-fire furnace. Much of this operation was illicit, tax-dodging. The area is proud of its renegade reputation, a haunt of smugglers and wreckers. Salt production was finally abandoned in the 1870s and the buildings became dwellings for oyster fishermen, before evolving into unfunded natural artworks.

We looked over the sharp ridges and reefs of an exposed Carboniferous limestone pavement that subverted any sense of scale. And then we came back, by sandy, sweet-smelling paths, through the magic twilight to the car. A black adder, about eighteen inches long, disturbed by our footfall, whipping back from the path into the undergrowth, left us arguing over its provenance. And symbolic meaning.

CULVER HOLE

Three youths on the loose at the end of summer. Putting on time before a new season. Gower. Port Eynon Point. Caught in that sometimes tight – *can't breathe, can't see* – sometimes elastic corridor between roaming free and watching, fearfully, where the next step must fall. A cave discussed by hostellers: *Culver Hole*. The repetition of those words, the meaningless, meaningful, mucky, spooky sound of it, is the looped undertow of our hard scramble around the limestone headland. *Culver Hole*. Rocks as grey as dental cement weathered into angled blades. Footholds: sandals slashed. Fingerholds. Toeholds. You wouldn't want to slip or slide or graze or puncture. Cavities and fantastic eroded spikes. Organisms thriving in the meanest of hollows, spits of colour as unfamiliar as the underside of a tongue.

Down below, cuts of light flash on shields of water. In rock pools with dangerously frayed edges, spumes of cloud are emerging photographic prints. Gower is a book of evidence to be read by geologists, out there with their hammers and knapsacks. Older sandstone layers thrusting upwards. The interaction of ice and fire, water and wind.

We were staying in the caravan. And it was good. Roger

took on the frying-pan cooking, when we didn't go down to the Ship Inn in Port Eynon. We cycled to Horton from Maesteg. We walked to the beach. We swam. We took out the rugby ball. We tried and tested the usual adolescent rivalries; improved anecdotes of shared experiences from the ridiculously short span of our early lives, tactfully managed zones of difference. But this Gower wasn't Dylan Thomas. It wasn't idyll, or paradise fondly remembered, summoned against present loss of powers: the squeeze of debt, afternoon blackouts, the nicotine sting of impertinent deadlines. Our caravan, anchored on brick, was set in an ordinary Welsh field with a panoramic spread forever tempting us to longer walks and what-lies-around-the-next-headland explorations. That place has vanished. Those times can never be retrieved by a magical necklace of sentences. No obliging village eccentrics took off their mildewed caps and set fire to their hair. I can't invent the banter of sassy girls on bicycles. Dylan Thomas broadcasts, those magazine commissions, are not archive. They come to life as they are told and they exist only in that telling, in the personality of the teller. And in the language-cast immortality of events that never happened in places that are always there.

In the story 'Who Do You Wish Was With Us?', Thomas calibrates the distance between Swansea and Gower by having one of his characters spit into his own hand: 'Still town grey.' The bus trip out through discriminations of semi-detached villas and neat bungalows brings the two excursionists as 'close as truants'. They want to be with laughing girls in 'open cricket shirts'. But they're happy to be tramping, unattached, down the long white road above

Oxwich Bay, in the shimmering mirage of one day's freedom from responsibility, with the sting and smell and bounced light of a 'fragmentary' sea. This is the tale of a hike advanced by jumping the Rhossilli bus. The walk is a ride and it doesn't matter because the young men are deposited on the 'humped and serpentine body' of Worm's Head. An accidental pilgrimage confirming them as townies. 'Let's climb down to the sea. Perhaps there's a cave with prehistoric drawings, and we can write an article and make a fortune.' They trade metaphors. If the day can't be written up, it never happened. 'A rock at the world's end' to which lies are brought and left in some spiky crack.

And the two of them talk about who they wish was with them. The third person on the track, witnessing the fall of the sun into the western ocean, is an absolute requirement. *Who do we wish was with us?* A woman older than we are now, but who will soon be the same age, then younger, much younger. Like the female archetype in Blake's strange cyclical pageant, *The Mental Traveller*. A witch dissolving to a 'Virgin bright'. To newborn babe. Lover. Crone. Over and over. On the same rocks. The binding, the cutting out of hearts. Figures carved on the walls of the cave. 'Labyrinths of wayward love.' Representations, in barest outline, follow natural flaws in the stone: lion, wolf, red deer, boar. In December 1989, when a fragment of antler was discovered in an alcove within Culver Hole cave, it seemed as though it had fallen into three-dimensional reality from a schematic drawing. Self-willed into existence. A tool with which to carve its own legend of eternal return.

We were gummed in the ordinary and the everyday. The thing that was to happen had not happened yet. I could say that Roger's father was a large man who owned and operated our small town's biggest (and only) department store. A man of committees and cabals. He had despatched his sons to an institution with charitable Methodist associations, the Leys School in Cambridge. J.G. Ballard, a former pupil, called his time in that town 'part of the continuum of strangeness' that made up his adolescence. A public school of this type, even one with pretensions to liberalism, was a constant reminder of Jimmy's earlier incarceration by the Japanese in Lunghua Camp. It took a figure as determined and self-starting as Ballard to make the best of Cambridge, its bookshops and cinemas. The enclosed society was just enough of a provocation to fire the perversity of his early fictions. I don't know what was achieved by my ten years sleepwalking in the narcoleptic daze of Cheltenham, among what was left of the retired colonels and the bat-eared spooks of the GCHQ eavesdropping station, but it was nothing good. The well-meant exile of caste privilege, which came with longer holidays than state schools, threw me together, for a couple of unprogrammed weeks, with Roger. We put aside our childhood street battles and differences of temperament to walk the circuit of the local hills. With dogs and guns.

Setting off now, on a cliff hike, without maps or plans or rucksacks, was where we were in life, at the border of the next thing, wondering just who we wanted to have with us.

The cave arrived quickly: beyond the shell of Salthouse cottages, across a section of limestone pavement, a wary climb over the first razor-toothed ridge of rock. If you looked back at Port Eynon Point at low tide, when that alien mass with its tessellation of smooth grey pebbles was exposed, with uneven patches of sand, trapped lagoons and pumice reefs that might once have been mountains, the headland was a pyramid embellished with striations like scars from a tribal initiation. Water did its work on porous stone, hollowing out secret places. Cracks. Crannies. Burrows. Mounds. A marine cemetery of crashed machines on a killing field that stretched as far as Ireland. A nightmare terrain in which calcified tanks were nudged aside by lumbering mastodons. A museum of broken metaphors and equivalents overwritten into existence. Soliciting silence.

Rock rose, marjoram, spiked speedwell, wild thyme: we register scents and shades of lime-loving plants we cannot name. It's early and heady, bacon and sausage, brown farm eggs and thick coarse bread sopping up the juices; lingering, caught-in-the-teeth aftertastes, and the hallucinogenic hit of new morning in a new place. We saunter, Indian file under the cliff, waist-high through bracken and springy grass. After the path has taken us as far as it chooses, out of sight of the familiar beach, we have to decide if we want to push on, crawling, abseiling, dropping down into every unpredictable chasm and slade, with no sense of when the tide will be rushing in. Or if we turn back, go through the woods to the quarry, to search out the mysterious cave they were talking about last night in the Port Eynon pub.

Culver Hole.

While we are still debating, another opportunity presents itself. The entrance to a cave we didn't expect is directly beneath the headland. It is black and rounded to the shape of some long extinct animal. A burrow furnished by limestone's fallibility. An invitingly smooth bore has been punched into the lichen-streaked wall at the end of a narrow inlet of pebbles, green pools and a morbidly blue conglomerate of mussel shells and hourglass sand. Along, on this remembered occasion, with a yellow plastic spade and a single rubber sandal. But this is not Culver Hole. This is a cave without a name. 'Port Eynon Point Cave' is the best the guidebook can

offer. Adding that the most effective view is obtained from Sedgers Bank. *Sedgers Bank*. What a title to conjure with! The residue of a sandbar enclosing a salt marsh protected from the sea by a fence of caulked timber.

In a characteristic poem, placing a melancholy traveller against a train window, W.G. Sebald writes about the difficulty of 'understanding the landscape'. The features the poet observes, and struggles to record, are watching the intruder as he is carried away. Terrain does not require the neurosis of language. We tie ourselves in such complicated knots trying to describe a thing that is all description. We confirm our own nuisance by employing, to greater or lesser effect, a redundant vocabulary of technical terms, overcooked epiphanies, showboating similes.

I'm not comfortable with catacombs, sewage outfalls, potholes, Tube tunnels or the clammy intestines of coastal caves. But I crawled into this one. Or did I? Am I confusing this episode with what happened later that morning at Culver Hole? When three male youths are out and about, there is constant pressure to confirm strengths and disguise weaknesses. I dragged behind when we cycled, hobbled by gears that ground and locked, oily chains that slipped their ratchets, slow punctures hissing in disgust at my incompetence. I came to hate the puff of trapped air that any touch on a valve releases. Walking was fine, dawn to dusk, at a steady, drink-it-all-in pace. None of us had a marker on caves. We were at the age of identifying survivable risks. And knowing that, for the moment, we were immortal.

You didn't go into that overwhelming darkness as easily as a flux of seawater over polished stones. You hauled yourself, on hands and knees, over hurdles of meat-cutting rock. The entrance was wide enough to be tempting, but this cave was more of a burrow than a cavernous smugglers' den out of Enid Blyton. The roof pressed down. Walls closed quickly in. Stooping became crawling. Blake's *Nebuchadnezzar*. Man-beast on all fours. In pain. Toes like claws. Light was borrowed. We were not equipped with a torch or matches. I squatted on the damp floor, drew up my knees and waited. The rock had its own muted soundtrack: dripping, contracting, breathing. *Groaning.* Swallowed echoes of remote and unremembered geological events. Excavations began in the nineteenth century, with the requirement to push back the biblically sanctioned timetable of creation, to confirm or refute Darwin. In this modest hole were found the remains of lion and bear. Dry bones, teased from the cave floor, were removed to a second burial, behind glass, in the dusty display cases of Swansea Museum. Handwritten labels, in ink as brown as blood, for a slaughtered Woolly Rhinoceros or ageing Mammoth with toothache: the midden detritus of feasts by our putative ancestors, the ones who passed through these places. Before they were places.

And the girls? Wait.

Culver Hole. Culver Hole. Culver Hole.

We were still chanting those words, failing to identify Iron Age forts, kicking at the scree of worked out quarries, half-hearing the sea bell off the point – and tracking the path, when it gave up, disappeared, dropped into a sudden cleft. It takes a professional, with the right instruments, time, helpers and budget, to appreciate the interaction of early humans, people of the last Ice Age, with these coops and cracks sculpted by water on limestone. Landscape is a harsh interrogation of trespassers who boast that a walk is its own justification. Anyone finding Culver Hole can see at once that it is unique, on this stretch of headland, in being a comparatively recent intervention; an effective, manmade adaptation of what was already there. The division in the rock wall has been bricked up with courses of the same grey-white stone set in lime mortar. Some of the bricks, near the top, have fallen away, allowing a point of access. There are recessive window-holes too: black, churchy, narrow, or round like portholes. The balance of window to wall is aesthetically satisfying. A geological fault has been exploited, and that can't have been an easy matter. Now Culver Hole is no hole. It is anti-hole. A wall waiting to be listed as architecture. A picture for the cover of the pink Landranger Ordnance Survey map, Number 159.

Culver Hole. *Culufre*. Culverhouse. Columbarium.

I wormed inside. And, this time, there was an inside. It was the antithesis of the first Port Eynon cave. There, you could enter without bending, before the mass closed down on you. Culver Hole was an illegitimate, wriggling intrusion – and then height, wet space, floors, stairways, ledges. *A columbarium.* Which is a fluttering pigeon chapel. A larder for living foodstuff, reserves against hard times. The stink of it had not quite saturated the stone. There were unfounded rumours of passages to the castle that once stood on the cliff above. Windows that were black outside, sucking in darkness, beams of marine light on votive niches and empty pigeon nooks.

Vernon Watkins, poet of Gower, played on the cave's associations with wreckers at the high tides of the equinox. His *Ballad of Culver's Hole* personifies place as legend: a sea-ghost returning, a revenant unwilling to shake free from the warm nimbus of memory.

> In a moment he has vanished.
> The gully's packed with dread.
> Where is he hiding in the rocks,
> The man they took for dead?

You can climb and you can fall. 'Danger haunts the upper ledge.' There are just so many times when you can step out of your knowledge and get away with it.

Emerging, lightheaded, on the cliff path, back with the gorse and the gulls, we fell in with three girls in shorts, tripping along in sandals that were never meant for venturing over sharp rocks. There were two sisters and their plainer cousin, holidaying in a Port Eynon caravan with their parents. I'm not sure how it works, but preferences soon become clear; where you walk on the narrow track, and who you reach down, in ways no longer acceptable, from a stile. Windsor Jones, a sociable and respected personality from a mixed grammar school in Maesteg, was in a relationship, going steady. He therefore entered into this competitive walk in an easy fashion, with no immediate agenda. Roger inserted himself alongside the elder sister, a dark bright cheerful girl it was all too easy to imagine in the framed future photograph, gown and mortarboard, that would soon be appearing on the family mantelpiece in Pontypridd, and justifying a few lines in the local paper. The younger sister was red-haired, spirited and not bothered about going to college. She'd been looking at pictures of Bardot. Ponytail and pout. Legs and gingham for wasting another night in a slow fisherman's pub. Lipstick-stained cigarette tweezed awkwardly between the tips of the fingers, as if it were too hot to handle. Rum and coke. And no jukebox to feed.

The distance to Rhossili would be six or seven miles, climbing, zigzagging into the next slade, down to hidden beaches and back up to the high cliff path. It was all talk, and wondering if they would make it; the cousin muttering darkly, the ginger girl with the freckles sharpening her tongue and questioning our airy assertion that there would be a bus at the end of it to carry us back home. Elemental aspects of the Gower coastline, the constantly shifting alignments of headlands, incline and syncline, were domesticated by the circumstances of the expedition, the rural monkey parade. The special habitat mosaic was a subtext to boiling adolescent hormones. The clever girl was clever enough to play down her geographic qualifications, all that she had read about igneous, metamorphic and sedimentary rocks. The plants that thrive in pockets of soil among the warm crevices of the cliffs.

The consensus was that they were too weary to follow the path down to Mewslade Bay, or to investigate the extruded neck of Worm's Head. Rhossili Beach could wait for another occasion, bus rides both ways. But the girls did come back, the next evening, after a drink in the pub, to the soft flattering gaslight of the Horton caravan.

VERNON WATKINS AT PENNARD

Vernon Watkins was a poet of symbol and cadence, all his instincts responsive to an established European tradition, but engaged and challenged by the place where he set himself, a modest bungalow on the eastern rim of Gower. A contemplative bus hop, lost in reverie, to the Swansea bank, where for years, refusing promotion, he manned a counter. The distance, around seven or eight miles of stop-start shuttle through countryside, village, suburb, was sufficient for decontamination; a misty-windowed limbo of processing between two quite distinct states of being. On one occasion, tasked with locking up at close of play, verses drumming in his head, he returned to his Pennard sanctuary, keys jangling, leaving the doors of Lloyd's Bank, Hospital Square, St Helen's Road, unsecured. The property was wide open, but unviolated. Poet's luck. A constable was despatched to track him to his private lair.

Early in 1961, I was supposed to meet Mr Watkins during his lunch break, for an hour of conversation in a local restaurant or café. It would probably have been Lovell's Café in St Helen's Road. The famed Kardomah, where the circle of Swansea poets, painters and talkers used to meet, was no longer there, a casualty of war. Vernon was unwell, at home in bed; our arrangements were changed.

There is a nicely composed photograph of Watkins at his counter. It demonstrates everything I missed that winter day: a grave, sharp-eared man carrying his lightweight three-piece suit with distinction. Neat, thick hair with side parting. Black fountain pen in hand, in a well-schooled grip. He addresses the official ledger as if it were a Matisse sketchbook or a fresh page on which to craft a poem of the sea. There is a residual melancholy in the wave-pattern frown lines, curve of eyebrows, closed lids. It looks very much as if the date is March 16 in any year, any century. A helmet-lamp, almost as large as the poet's tipped avian skull, descends: a cone of artificial light focused precisely on the zone of work. Sun-shafts from our right emphasise the bank worker's shoulder, the silvery hair. The rest of the trappings are out of Dickens or Kafka: brass inkwell, scales, frosted glass partition, gridded prison window.

After dropping out of Cambridge, where he featured as a figure of fun in *Lions and Shadows*, the fashionable novel by his contemporary, Christopher Isherwood, and setting aside the thrust of career and a period of spiritual crisis in Cardiff, Watkins settled to his hometown routine: as little responsibility as could be managed with just enough security to keep a roof over the head of wife and family. And to secure his Pennard retreat, where he bounded down precipitous paths through prickly gorse, on long, light summer evenings, to Hunt's Bay or Pwlldu.

Vernon Watkins was a bank employee of lower status than his editor at Faber, T.S. Eliot, who worked for Lloyd's in the foreign exchange department. Watkins didn't chafe, like the

poet of *The Waste Land*, beneath the pavements of Lombard
Street in the City of London. Eliot was nagged by Ezra
Pound, tormented by the heels of typists as they clattered
overhead, while he waited on the dead sound of the final
stroke of the bell of Hawksmoor's St Mary Woolnoth. But he
recognised Watkins' qualities early and remained a supporter
even when sales figures flatlined. The Pope of Russell Square
respected the commitment, in an unforgiving era, to poetry

as the sacred flame. Immortal whispers of unacknowledged hierophants.

I was a schoolboy, landed with a project, and letting it drift in fits and starts, with no proper understanding as yet how the specifics of place would supply narrative structure, materials with which to confect a mythology of borrowed fragments. The idea was to produce a paper on Dylan Thomas that would nudge me into Cambridge by a side door. It was never going to work. I had no faith in what I produced, but the doing of it was an adventure, a model for much that followed: tracking down witnesses, walking around potentially significant territory, taking photographs, scribbling notes. My rivals in this scholarship business delivered immaculately presented typescripts in glassine folders, with pages of footnotes, bibliographies, citations. My sorry gathering looked as if it had been on the road for months. It was sprawlingly handwritten in blue ink, with revisions, and lifted only by a collection of tipped-in snapshots. The mentors of the scheme groaned. And were visibly astonished when I was the only one from the school to go forward to a final selection board. I thought I made a mess of the preliminary interview in Bristol, but my nervy improvisations must have been mistaken for a form of integrity. Or light relief from the full-frontal assaults of future champions of breakfast conferences with their bullet-point presentations and rehearsed responses to every challenging bouncer.

I didn't do myself any favours in Cambridge. I tried to change the time of the interview so that I could play in a rugby match. This was not appreciated. The inquisition sat in Magdalene, the college where Watkins read modern languages, and where he left without completing his degree. When I was asked if I could quote a few lines of Dylan Thomas, I launched into 'A Refusal to Mourn the Death, by Fire, of a Child in London', which I had by heart. And which I muttered to myself as I took the train from Liverpool Street to Cambridge. 'Never until the mankind making. . .'

They stopped me. 'No, no, no. That's not Thomas.'

I was dumfounded, confused, knocked out of my stride. The anecdotes of Laugharne and Cwmdonkin Park dried up. It was over. When I showed the paper to my English teacher in Cheltenham, Jim Greenwood, he told me that I needed to make more of the visit to Vernon Watkins. That was the money shot. How did I get there? What was the setting? Establish his physical presence, his conversation beyond the matter of his relationship with Dylan Thomas. I had to do more than merely confirm the versions trotted out in all the biographic memoirs and festschrifts. He was right. But what he wanted was beyond me, and there was no time.

I came back to Magdalene, many years later, to deliver a lecture. The walk down Bridge Street to the Cam, and the entrance through the porters' lodge, had that remembered mood of a condemned man waiting to be sentenced. The shame of the original episode lingered and had to be set aside. Ghostly inquisitors were still marking my talk with red pencils and offering payment in the ritual humiliation of high table. 'That's not Thomas. No, no, no.'

*

I stood, in the dark, on the narrow road that ran above the unseen but sonorously present bay, trying to make out the names of scattered, out-of-season bungalows. I wanted *The Garth, West Cliff.* I was parked some distance off, near *Heatherslade*, a three-bedroom clifftop villa that had once been the Watkins family home, before they departed for Cardiff, and later an extensive property on Caswell Bay, with tennis court beside the beach. Of course I didn't know that. Or much else, beyond what I had read, trawled from the usual sources; published memoirs and the Dylan Thomas gathering, *Letters to Vernon Watkins.* Which Watkins had introduced. There were no letters from Vernon, although he had written plenty of them, enclosing solicited notes and coins, and helping, when requested, with revisions of poems and other editorial tasks. The point being that Vernon kept moderately chaotic files from the time he left Swansea to join the RAF in December 1941. He honoured every word that arrived from his wayward friend, while Thomas scattered incoming correspondence to the winds. One letter to Vernon, however, was found by Gwen, after the war, at the bottom of a discarded kitbag.

Some of my mother's Morriston cousins, aunts, uncles, taught alongside D.J. Thomas, Dylan's father, in Swansea Grammar School. Nieces were always appearing in revivals of *Under Milk Wood* with amateur and semi-professional players in Mumbles. (The kind of scene Kingsley Amis enjoyed sending up.) They knew Vernon Watkins and had been involved in performances of *Ballad of the Mari Lwyd*, that haunting year's-end masque, in which the importunate and excluded dead rattle on double-bolted doors, for access to food and fire. 'White Horse of the Sea . . . The Dead return.' My relatives brokered the introduction to Watkins, the lunchtime meeting that never happened. But Vernon was generous enough, despite his sickness, to invite me to come, that evening, to his home.

The Gower poet is sitting up in a bed that does not seem big enough for two, wearing what I might misremember as a cricket blazer. Do we sip a dry sherry? Probably not. Perhaps a mug of tea? Gwen Watkins is in attendance, weighing up the scale of nuisance, interested in, if sceptical of, the benefits of my intrusion. The Dylan story, in the eight years since his death, has become a burden. Old scars have not yet healed: the way, for example, Thomas chose not to appear at St Bartholomew's Church in Smithfield, to undertake his duties as best man at the Watkins wedding. A role that I performed, in the same place, many years later, for another poet, Brian Catling. Gwen recalled that day in wartime. 'The Lady Chapel had many pictures and articles stored in its back pews,' she told me, 'but Vernon bought a great sheaf of golden roses for the altar, and we had candles because electricity had to be cut off, so all very romantic.'

Later, with five children and a household to run on a bank clerk's inadequate salary, along with whatever 'honorarium' alms accrued from poetry, Gwen came to resent the financial support posted to Dylan – who earned more, on and off, and left most of it in the pubs and clubs of Soho and Fitzrovia. I have a grasp, decades too late, on how the process of writing, discovering paradigms that are already there, is a negotiation between a long-cohabiting couple. The fruits of a revived and tested intimacy. Gwen's cutting edge, if I presume to understand it, grew from the knowledge that whatever emerged from Vernon's study, at night, at the end of his copious siftings and soundings, his attempts at imposing shape on the fugitive music that came so easily, the subtle cadences of his work, *issued from her*. She brought her intelligence, her ambitions, her physical reality, to this partnership. As an unacknowledged dowry. And it should be recognised. Vernon, in the crisis of his Cardiff breakdown, the 'revolution of sensibility' as he called it, was fragile. But fragile like a mountain goat trembling on one boulder's edge, before leaping to the next. There is the famous story of Dylan, cackling with delight, when Vernon stumbled, after a rare night on the piss in the Chelsea wartime blackout, over a troublesome obstacle. A forbidden sliver of torchlight revealed one small black feather.

'Now that I am at the beginning of my '90s,' Gwen reported, 'I feel the urge to write about my childhood in my grandmother's house. Of which I have a clearer memory than any other house I have lived in.' So was I wrong about the bed, the cricket blazer? 'Your memory of Vernon receiving you in bed is strange to me,' Gwen said, 'as I could never get him to even rest in an armchair.' The poet was at his desk or on the move. 'He must have been very ill to do that. I have seen him in the grip of an appalling asthma attack, struggling along the West Cliff in a bitter wind, to get to the bus, to go to work.' The doctor in Seattle, who performed the autopsy, after Vernon died on the tennis court, could not believe that with a heart in that condition the visiting poet could even break into a jog. But the former bank clerk, out there with three younger men, was winning the set when his seizure came.

They met, Vernon and Gwen, at Bletchley Park. Watkins had been an unlikely and unmartial sergeant in the RAF police, before he was transferred to Intelligence. He went out of his way, like a public-school prefect promoted for academic standing, but not expected to actually perform normal duties, to avoid taking disciplinary action. Code breaking among a squabble of ludicrously over-qualified eccentrics. The carry-on-Cambridge hijinks, now being heritaged into contention for Hollywood Oscars, was a useful preparation for future life as a hermetic, Neo-Platonist poet. 'I have been taught the script of the stones, and I know the / tongue of the wave.' The Watkins poem 'Taliesin in Gower', from his collection *The Death Bell*, is a decoding of elements of the founding myth of place. Geology hides fossil traces of the first people, and the magic by which they appeased the ominously encrypted skies. 'Unicorn-spiral shell secreting the colours / of day.'

Propped up on his pillows, febrile, bright of eye, Watkins was courteous, answering questions he must have fielded so many times as if they were fresh minted. And then taking the trouble to sound me out, to discover what I was *really* after once this smokescreen task was done. We could have sat, comfortably, in silence, in the dim light, for the interval that Gwen allowed. Before her hovering presence made it clear that *the door was over there*.

When the poet died, too early, his widow became a scrupulous editor of his papers; coming, at last, to value midnight pages that took such a toll on their life together. Memories became books, accounts were settled, old wounds picked over. *Portrait of a Friend*, first published in 1983, became *Dylan Thomas: Portrait of a Friend* on its reissue, somewhat revised, in 2005. It was floated on a rising tide of Celtic Dylan-mania. Heritage-broker bureaucrats and gaudy pamphleteers realised that the bad boy's name could be turned to advantage as a room for breakfast meetings in revamped marina hotels, or a toad-squat statue, a festival prompt: a heavy cultural industry to rival coal. With Vernon gone, Gwen moved into a large house in Oxford, where she rented a room to Dr Ruth Pryor, scholar and bibliographer, editor of posthumous Watkins collections.

In the quiet moments, when the thin walls seemed to close in around us, I looked at the framed photographs; especially the one of Dylan and Caitlin Thomas with croquet mallets. The turf is coarse. The gorse bank in the background is as knotted and wild as the hair of the curly poet and his golden wife. I read this charming snapshot as confirmation of true friendship, and an unrescinded benediction for this ground, the grass carpet between the bungalow and the drop to Hunt's Bay. But it was not quite what it seemed: the double portrait was taken on the lawn at *Heatherslade*, the old Watkins family house. Dylan, in short leather golfing jacket and polo neck, a visiting Chelsea bohemian, propping the handle of the mallet against his private parts, with suggestive grip of hands, and foot firmly on ball, is a playful performer. Caitlin, in flowery summer dress with white bib collar, is standing a little apart. She is round-cheeked, full-figured, in girlish ankle socks and strappy sandals. There is the flicker of a smile for the photographer. The implication being that at any moment now the loving, raging, impossible couple will be cracking

each other over the head. The *Heatherslade* idyll on the lawn is the half-time truce in a battle still unresolved at the time of the poet's premature, choking death in New York City.

Gwen made it quite clear, even then, that she never really

liked Dylan. There was too much to forgive. But, like so many others, she was dazzled by the aura of Dylan's wife: the transmutation of all that boiling anger. Mrs Watkins told the biographer Paul Ferris that Caitlin was a bird of paradise, proud of her body, quick to take her clothes off on a beach. 'Gwen remembers her bathing at Foxhole, a bay near Swansea,' Ferris wrote, 'skin shimmering with light, red-gold hair prismatic in the sun, cornflower-blue eyes, apple-blossom cheeks that you felt you wanted to stroke. She was like Blodeuwedd, the woman made of flowers.'

'Apple-blossom cheeks.' 'Woman made of flowers.' Symbols from *The Mabinogion* and J.G. Frazer, Jane Harrison, Robert Graves and David Jones, infusing this landscape, were making themselves known to me. Owl. Cave. Shroud. Darkness at noon. Solar flares locked in stone. Occulted sun. The Gwen Watkins memoir has a photograph of a bloated, halfcut, idiot-smirking Dylan as its frontispiece. Here is revenge on the magic of the immortally youthful bohemians on the *Heatherslade* lawn. Now the thickening and corrupted poet is swaddled in layers of interview-clothes picked from the wrong model in the window of the Fifty Shilling Tailors. Dylan has bridled his own mouth, on the print sent to the Watkins family, by scribbling a single, black-ink word: *Fool*. Gwen's caption is: 'A bulging Apple among poets. . .'

Adequately swotted up for the Dylan Thomas part of my interview, I was underprepared for conversation with Vernon Watkins. I had read the one-way traffic of the *Letters* and paid close attention to Vernon's linking notes and introduction. I appreciated the tactful job he made of a foreword doing its best for the slim pickings of the aborted *Adventures in the Skin*

Trade. But I knew Vernon's poetry only through anthology pieces. And one in particular from 'The Broken Sea', included in Kenneth Allott's *Contemporary Verse*, published by Penguin in 1950. The pages of my copy were tanned and had a smell I associated with poetry fixed on yellowing wartime paper. A few lines of biographical information in italic. And then the chosen verse. 'A seawave plunges. Listen. Below me crashes the bay.' Contributors were presented in chronological order. I registered that Watkins was older than Betjeman, Empson, Auden, George Barker, Dylan Thomas, David Gascoyne.

I told Mr Watkins that I hoped to go to Dublin and he recalled his visit to Yeats. Where Dylan Thomas, in his prose, drew on Joyce, with the playful titling of *Portrait of the Artist as a Young Dog* and the nightwork incantation of *Under Milk Wood*, Watkins was under the spell of Yeats: as poet, magus, conduit to Blake and Swedenborg. In the poem *Yeats in Dublin*, composed as a memorial, Watkins has his mentor murmuring: 'The young poets toil too much . . . Till nothing but the grit is left.' Lofty Parnassian pronouncements, and talk of laying something out 'on the table' for dissection, sound very much like a cut at Eliot and *Prufrock*. The recapitulation of this Dublin encounter in the 'long, amber room' was offered, now, as validation of my choice: to spend my student years in the seatown of Yeats and Joyce – another Swansea, another long curve of bay, as Watkins suggested.

It was gracefully done, making it clear that the nuisance of young men knocking on the doors of established poets was an honourable tradition. And there was something in this too about avoiding the boil and heave of London or the tempting spaces of the USA, where Dylan Thomas came to grief. But those difficult places are a necessary rite of passage. 'Without the subtlety London taught,' Yeats says, 'I could not learn to speak.' *Yeats in Dublin* is a model for striking a record of such a meeting: conversation recalled, characters established. A significant memory is confirmed in sinewy verse. The filtered light and washed-out colour of Dublin dissolves into harsher Gower. 'And the threads, threads, threads of the sea.' Beckettian footfall on black shingle, on shale and hard scrabbled stones.

THE COTTAGE HOSPITAL, MAESTEG

Our low-lit, flickering poetry séance was done, it was time to speak of cricket. Vernon Watkins was born in Maesteg, the town where I grew up. My mother had been born in the same place, one year earlier. Vernon's father, transferring from bank to bank as his status rose, took his family to Bridgend, then Swansea, before he moved out to Gower, and retirement at Pennard. Vernon was sent, as I had been, to an English public school. He followed Christopher Isherwood, two years ahead of him, to Repton in Derbyshire. The final eighteen months of his expensive incarceration seem to have been a golden time; spent reading Keats, Shelley and Rupert Brooke. And confirming his identity as a poet who played tennis. His father, so it is said, settled on Repton when, driving there for his first inspection, he found the tennis courts in lively occupation.

Sitting up in bed, Watkins traded recollections of cricket matches at St Helens, a short step from the bank. He spoke of the great days of Glamorgan's championship-winning team of 1948: Wilf Wooller, Muncer, Hever, Parkhouse, Willie Jones, Emrys Davies, Allan Watkins. Tennis remained a passion. He played hockey, he said. And told me to continue turning out for Bridgend.

After thanking my hosts, I stepped into the gathering darkness, to pick my way back along the cliff path.

Shortly after this meeting I began to acquire the Watkins collections published by Faber; most, going back to the late forties and early fifties, were still in their first editions. I soon realised how powerfully the place where Vernon lived informed the coded structure of his verse. Meic Stephens in his *New Companion to the Literature of Wales* speaks of Watkins as 'a modern metaphysical' tapping 'insight-symbols from the Gower shoreline'. Summoning the bard Taliesin, almost as John Cowper Powys channelled and re-invented him for his own purposes in *Porius*, Watkins inducts the demiurge into a world immediately visible from his window: 'I witness here in a vision the landscape to which I was born.' He solicits the moment that is all moments, with secular time as an element through which the poet, in a heightened state of consciousness, after migrating across a set of numinous territorial markers, animates the Platonic 'replica'. The act of nocturnal verse-making, for the poet of place, is a willed abdication of originality. A wearing away of egoic interference. A oneness with the indifferent gods of rock and wave.

From the start, from all those reports of Vernon, in his long tennis shorts, skipping from rock to rock, poetry was contrived as a statement of belonging. 'Late I return . . . My country is here.' But the returnee, the eternal revenant of ballads named after the geographical features of the Gower Peninsula, is already dead: drowned, picked clean. Hidden for centuries in the winch of a cave. 'These stones are prayers; every boulder is hung on a breath's / miraculous birth.' Suicided pilgrims. Wrecked ships. Walkers making the same futile, questing journey, time after time. With no resolution. No release. 'Swollen shoes, a pole and a pack.'

The Australian poet Peter Minter, writing about Charles Olson's Promethean attempt to forge an epic of place, travelling all ways at once along the curvature of time, out from the fishing port of Gloucester, Massachusetts, finds parallels in the dream-maps of Aboriginal people. He quotes the cultural theorist Howard Morphy: 'Aboriginal paintings can only be fully understood as maps once it is realised that the criterion for inclusion is not topographical but mythological and conceptual; paintings are thus representations of the totemic geography.'

Poetry of the Gower dreamtime, crafted by Vernon Watkins, is a poetry of origin, in which named sites – caves, cliffs, headlands, bays – have meaning only because they belong to a Christian-pantheist memory-map of ancestors who have become places. 'Stone Footing', an act of listening, is a key text.

Stopping my ears to Venus and her doves,
I steal stone footing, find death's carved decree;
I choose the path, the rock which no man loves
Familiar to birds, cast by a barren sea.
Cold on this ridge among the breeding winds,
Starved in the famine forced by Adam's rib,
Here I hold breath, knowing the door of my friends
Is rock, and I am exiled from their tribe.
I put my ear to the ground, I plant my foot
Against grey rock, but wind and seawave smother
The stone's coiled fossil-saga; this navel-knot
Fastens my moving to the great rock-mother.
I would unchain them; but there flies that other
Bearing the sea, and kills me with her shot.

I went to Dublin. I read Charles Olson and engaged with his theory of 'open field' poetics. The west of Ireland was not west enough, we were intoxicated by taller waves, wider spaces; desert wilderness, road writers, new sounds. When I became editor of the university literary magazine, I solicited a contribution from Vernon Watkins, who was generous enough to send his 'Postscript' after the assassination of Jack Kennedy. My letter was a clumsy attempt to respect those early Welsh influences, while sketching more recent and louder affiliations. Where there was common ground, I missed it.

Newly married, living quietly on the Mediterranean island of Gozo, I laboured over film scripts and documentaries that would never be made. One of these was an unsolicited

television adaptation of the verse play, *Ballad of the Mari Lwyd*, by Vernon Watkins. The germ of the drama is the classic Watkins conceit of the returning dead, cold rhymers at the door. The folk background, with its shamanic tracings, had some relationship with Maesteg; or, more specifically, the hilltop village of Llangynwyd, and the thirteenth-century church of St Cynwyd, where my parents were married and where I was christened. On one of the regular outings with my mother and great-aunt, by local bus, then what seemed to a child like a long puff up a winding hill, to pay our respects to my grandmother, to scrub and polish ancestral graves, and sustain a dialogue with the perky and unquiet dead, we bumped into a family connection who still lived in the village. And we were invited to take tea in a whitewashed cottage with low ceilings, dark inside, where the horse's skull was kept. This was the Mari Lwyd: 'Horse of Frost, Star-horse, and White Horse of the Sea'. In traditional practice, the skull was buried, before being excavated on New Year's Eve, to be

ribboned and processed by rhyming drunks and mummers, house to house. A ritual not unlike the ploughboys' wild parade with a Straw Bear, attended by blackface Molly gangs in travesty, in the fen country beyond Peterborough. 'Give us coins and sustenance or face the consequences.'

The Llan skull was carved grey wood. I believe that it is now in a folk museum. The memory stayed with me. While T.S. Eliot, the other banker/poet, slummed with Marie Lloyd, the feisty Cockney music-hall headliner from Hackney, Watkins went back to the death-dance of Mari Lwyd, which he described as: 'This ancient custom, traceable perhaps to the White Horse of Asia.' Or an outline cut in a chalk hillside, close to the flinty Ridgeway.

We cycled to Victoria, the capital of Gozo, to catch the early market, and sometimes to search for an outdated copy of *The Times*. Reading the obituary page, once I'd done with the sports section, I learned that Vernon Watkins had died. And that he shared a birthday with Anna, my new wife. He had taken his retirement package, along with a few late honours, and followed Dylan Thomas across the Atlantic, and then the whole North American continent, to a place that would give him time to rest, consider and look back. Produce new work for new gods.

There was a strategic element to this project, my Vernon Watkins script. Richard Burton and Elizabeth Taylor had taken shares in the new Welsh television franchise, Harlech. I gambled that somebody in the organisation would be deputed to come up with light cultural topdressing with a Welsh pedigree. I sent off the script and was invited to Cardiff. They were surprised by my youth, but this was a better interview. 'How much do you need to do it?' *Do it?* I thought I could pass the thing over, pick up the cheque. Such a situation never arose again. I fled. The poem stayed with me. 'Rigor mortis straightens the figure.' I walked away and kept on walking. The next Gower expedition, a return to Port Eynon, was the exorcism.

ALBION ISLAND VORTEX

The car hauls a thick slice of Hackney to the deserted, out-of-season Port Eynon car park. An unguarded border post on the periphery of the rocks and caves. My companion, the poet and sculptor Brian Catling, is London bred and branded; a South of the River man on the move. Dark hair hangs loose over his forehead. Thin, round spectacles. A sock of beard cultivated in a student-artisan style that went out of fashion after the arrest of Peter Sutcliffe. Collarless shirt. Labourer's blue donkey jacket. Leather gloves striking a sinister note. But the season calls for them: January 4, 1973.

Inspecting the photocopied sheets that served as a catalogue for *Albion Island Vortex,* a show of work brought to the Whitechapel Gallery from a range of British Places (Gower, North Wales, Dorset, New Forest, Yorkshire, Cheviot Hills), it seems that I did the Port Eynon to Worm's Head walk, alone, on December 28, 1972. And then, fired by what I had discovered, I returned with Catling early in the New Year. In that heady period when our first books were appearing, there was an impulse to map out a dreamtime appropriate to our abilities, such as they were. We read widely, eclectically, across the disciplines, snacking and sampling among established authorities and soon-to-be-forgotten weirdos, before – in my case – coming back to David Jones, *The White Goddess* by Robert Graves, *A Vision* by W.B. Yeats. And William Blake. Always Blake. Blake and London. Blake and the stones. 'All things begin and end in Albion's Druid rocky shore.' I was as mystified and intrigued by the cosmologies explored in Blake's *Milton* as by the abstract elegance, unreadable as cuneiform, of the equations in *The Large Scale Structure of Space–Time* by S.W. (Stephen) Hawking and G.F.R. Ellis, which was published by Cambridge University Press in 1973. Hackney Central Library (later a music venue, now a cinema) held a copy.

Blake anticipated my thirst for Gower. Coming right out of the crucible of Lambeth particulars, he pushed me west. 'The Sea of Time & Space thunder'd aloud against the rock.'

BLAKE'S COTTAGE, FELPHAM

But beyond Blake's diagram of 'The Mundane Egg' – a dreamtime map if there ever was one – I was fascinated by Plate 29 of *Milton*, where a falling star is about to spear the heel of WILLIAM, as he arches backwards in convulsive, ecstatic spasm, wearing a pair of loose drawers, as if surprised on his way to the beach at Felpham. I was taken with what Jeremy Prynne said about the poet arranging for this 'genetic interchange' with the immortal spirit of Milton, in order to revise the errors of *Paradise Lost*. The episode had to happen *outside* London, in a cottage garden, between sea and hills, when Blake and his wife lived beyond their knowledge for the first and last time.

In a lecture on Charles Olson's *Maximus IV, V, & VI*, given at Simon Fraser University in Vancouver, on July 27 1971, Prynne calls *Paradise Lost* 'a great angelic history'. He is preoccupied, after an evening re-reading Olson's poem in preparation for this talk, with the current status of histories, cosmologies, the concept of the voyage. 'The universe considered as a whole . . . That means that the universe is already the most completely prime particular thing.' *Already*. Before the pre-Socratic philosophers worried at its outline. Before there was outline. Before Newton. Or Blake. Or Milton. 'Some people can get it just like that from the night sky.' The clarity of the pinpricks and patterns of remote light coming back to us, with original brilliance, on these Gower ridges. At this season. The grudging turn of the year.

And being where he was, in troubled hibernation, in a rented cottage beside the English Channel, Blake 'decides to re-work Milton and to arrange for the demonic possession of himself by Milton.' Which is a risky but noble procedure.

And a great metaphor for what is attempted, at the crudest level, by parking ourselves in this Port Eynon field and setting out, cameras and notebooks primed, on this walk. The dumb realisation that *place is poem*. Identifying, like fully paid-up Romantics, some authentic wilderness, a rapture of gaze, is not our task. You don't bring experience home like a souvenir. You listen and learn. You *confirm*. The walk does not require the walker. If we catch even the barest glimmer of the fear in the cave, the hunger, we will come closer to appreciating the blind gamble that one act, or invented ritual, must bring about a benevolent configuration of the planets. That is how Prynne concludes his lecture, with the notion that Stonehenge and Avebury were 'chance shots'. 'Sooner or later it must come round again . . . They didn't know. They just wanted it. That's how it happened . . . Then you have the particular condition of transpiring through the noble arc, from the land to the shore, from the shore to the sea, from the sea to the ocean, from the ocean to the void, from the void to the horizontal curve, which is love. You have the condition. You turn it round. You bring it all back in. You come right down, and you are home.'

Home. Yeats advised Synge to go to a wild island off the Galway coast and to study its life because that life 'had never been expressed in literature'. And never needed to be. Gower and its caves have been expressed time and again, by poets, painters and naturalists. What they are all trying to approach is something like Blake's chart of time and space, his 'Mundane Egg', inside which man can incubate and re-enter Eternity. 'From Zenith to Nadir in midst of Chaos.' That is to say, a total vision. Revealed in a few lines on a page. An ink mark, the Shell of the Egg, on which living flesh can grow.

My hiking companion, Brian Catling, an operator smart enough to store his provisional discoveries for decades, hit on an evolutionary chain around this time: limestone reef, animal spine, hunter's bow. When he came, in the new millennium, to release prose works held under pressure for forty years, they spouted forth in a rush of ten immense fictions (and counting), delivered over a six-year period. Epics of unfettered imagination. Distorted fever-histories predicated on legends of place and triumphantly mangled.

The original product of this late flowering was *The Vorrh*, called by Alan Moore 'the current century's first landmark work of fantasy'. But that sure-footed opening is no fantasy. The mythic bow derived from our Worm's Head walk, buried for so long, makes its inevitable return. A weapon, carved from a woman's peeled spine, is carried 'into the wilderness'. Prophecy, as Prynne asserts, is about having the nerve to wait. 'Seers die,' Catling writes, 'in a threefold lapse, from the outside in.'

The radiant curve of bone, this future weapon, a transmitter anchored to Overton Cliff, is already there in 1973, in the spidery needlepoint drawing the Camberwell sculptor made after returning from our expedition. The drawing was exhibited in the Whitechapel show. Catling supplied a poem-note, under the rubric 'Astronomer's Rib'.

Under wind dome, fallen land wing
cast among bone maps of haunted skins.
Acid runs of ice compression blister
life along white calcium wounds.
Broken joints, snapped tendril star spines
hooked through tundra gut. Ice shrinks
back, hanging vegetation swamps upholstered
rock. It is to be injected by broken needles
into iron-clad profiles, sacred under
time-bore moons.

A signifier for that period, 1973, the era when – as I demonstrated – late-hippie moustaches were about to be

replaced by the stern cavalry droop of the missing Lord Lucan, was that we set out from Port Eynon, not with a decent Ordnance Survey map but with a badly drawn copy of Blake's 'Mundane Egg' diagram. A cosmology of overlapping planetary circuits of influence with the Egg as a 'vast Concave Earth'. Cutting, like the tail of a comet across the firmament, is 'Milton's Track', as he leaves Eternity and journeys 'above the rocky masses'.

Tramping off down the overgrown path towards the first headland was a gesture at initiation or reintegration with home territory. The Gower walk was my attempt at a 'genetic interchange' with salt, stone, plant, bird. There was blind trust that we would locate Goat's Hole Cave at Paviland, and the radon traces of the Red Lady, simply because we wanted it. Because the Red Lady was already an important splinter in my mythology of place.

Being established in London, owning a terraced Hackney house, having casual employment in Whitechapel and Wapping, floated the memories of my first Gower walk closer to the surface. But now it was a map tattooed on my back, out of sight, rubbing against a poisoned shirt. The projected songline was brighter all the time, for belonging to an elective exile. As a returnee, I was like one of the cold wraiths in a Vernon Watkins ballad. Catling's Overton Mere drawing looked as if it had been *literally* tattooed with a sharp needle into pliant paper: dots, pinpricks, fissures.

Publishing through my own small press gave me a measure of control over output. As well as a conscious attempt to register London places and local specifics, the somatic undertow tugged me back to Wales. In a book from 1972 called *Muscat's Würm*, I referenced the last European Ice Age. The sections were given titles from a chart of coal levels in the Maesteg mine where my maternal grandfather worked. 'Middle Black Band' was excavated from family dreams, as they were netted in the roots and branches of a remembered oak tree. Genealogy became an instrument, an aspiration. To pretend that we are not quite lost. And alone. 'Black glass of ancestor time / scratched with a needle.' One of the poems, 'Red Chamber, Yellow Top', was derived from Gower caves I had yet to visit. The chill, the watching and waiting on the edge of a future sea, came from a brief inspection of the excavated bones in Swansea Museum.

so that we hugged to the apron
this cold
and had no urge for other

what we found in the ice
we ate and were sick

worshipped the sudden brightness
above the hills

not understanding nor seeking, this

The whole drift of a subsequent book, *The Birth Rug*, published in 1973, after the second Gower walk, and after the birth of our first daughter, worried against the rocks of origin. 'A hut of words primitive to our nature.' There is steady pressure to rise above a desired topography and to engage, at the same time, with the bloody imperatives of human existence.

eye stops down to zero: here
ice striates, drags, fails

pulls back on an iron menagerie,
crusted necropolis stage set

where the last of them crouched
facing south, the warm valley

To become 'immersed in an element, not splashed corrosively' was the challenge laid down by Prynne, in a letter responding to these books. To make an adequate exchange. To engage, fully, and not to pass through a corridor of images, bearing off trophies, splashes of trapped light. I was greedy in the wrong way. Too sure that we would make it back, at the end of the day's adventure, to the car.

I was twenty-nine-years-old at the time of the Gower walk, Catling a few years younger. I met him when I was teaching a film class in Walthamstow, after the senior tutor, a Jewish-American leftist, victim of the McCarthy blacklist, had suffered a complete collapse. Brian was his own man. He knew what he wanted and he was a self-starter. He arrived at the class with films in the can, following up on rumours of a strange young teacher handing out cameras and stock, while preparing for a future career as a cultural 'freak-wrangler'. All the loose cannons slouched in and slumped. All the mature students with seething, unfulfilled projects. I set them up and turned them loose into London.

Soon afterwards, dabbling in Blakean shallows, we began to map out lines of influence through a series of walks across England and Wales. Winchester to the New Forest to Salisbury. Streatley-on-Thames, down the Ridgeway, to Avebury, and back along the Kennet and Avon Canal. Salisbury to Glastonbury and Cadbury Castle. I had the chart of the Cathedral Cities from S. Foster Damon's *A Blake Dictionary*, with its pattern of dotted lines and unsuspected triangulations, somewhere at the back of my mind. We explored the Welsh borders and the Black Mountains and stretches of the South Wales coastline. I climbed Cader Idris. Before we rounded the series off with a tramp, sleeping in woods and ditches, to Chichester. And Blake's cottage at Felpham. 'In Felpham I heard and saw the Visions of Albion.'

The third party in the show at the Whitechapel Gallery, exposing some of the material derived from these expeditions, was Laurence 'Renchi' Bicknell. His walks were more substantial: out of the door in Hackney and down, by river, road, forest, hill, doss house and ditch, with no maps, no equipment, to Swansea. Boat to Cork. On to a rocky

cove in the west of Ireland. And a boosted visionary release that fed back into his paintings. Even when the details of the journal of that walk were obliterated and the parts of himself he no longer required, carried away from London, were erased.

Renchi followed this with a twenty-four-day yomp along the 'Michael and Mary' lines, from Hopton on Sea in Norfolk to St Michael's Mount in Cornwall. He kept an illustrated diary of this walk and published it, in Blakean tribute, as an illuminated book. He was scrupulous in footnoting the relevant geology (motor to his dreaming): 'East to West Silurian basement with Mendip limestone, crossed North to South by golden oolitic limestone line from Lincoln to Golden Cap.'

After we had circumambulated London's Orbital Motorway, the M25, and followed in John Clare's weary footsteps from Dr Matthew Allen's Epping Forest asylum to his home village, north of Peterborough, Renchi completed his exemplary set of English pilgrimages by making 'Seven Synchronised inner and outer journeys particularly honouring William Blake's visual rendition of John Bunyan's *The Pilgrim's Progress*'. The journeys were celebrated by another illuminated booklet, for which he learned how to make etchings on copper. The relevance to my sequence of Gower walks, undertaken over decades with no formal plan, is explained by Renchi's introductory note, in which he posits 'the Archetypal Journey' that anchors, consciously or unconsciously, the pattern of his life. He suggests that three long pilgrimages are required stages in the attempt to achieve enlightenment or resolution. 'Firstly, from London to Swansea when I was 27, leading to my Schoolhouse Vision. Secondly, along the Michael Line from Hopton on Sea in Norfolk to Carn Lês Boel in Cornwall. And thirdly, and continuously in this series, from Boston in Lincolnshire to Abbotsbury in Dorset.' Other walks – around Mount Arunachala, the Isle of Avalon, and counterclockwise around Mount Annapurna and the M25 – become part of a synchronistic process.

The inspiration for Renchi's third journey was a book by Gerda S. Norvig, *Dark Figures in the Desired Country (Blake's Illustrations to The Pilgrim's Progress)*. So the chain stretches, as Renchi engages with Norvig's reading of Blake's 're-visioning' of Bunyan's *The Pilgrim's Progress*. And the process of extracting archetypal material from the solitary pilgrim's testing march, as he digs into the spiral of Christian's assault on the sacred mount and the eidetic glint from the shining city on the hill. Walks overlap and interweave in marginal tracery. Renchi accompanies his father on a sixty-kilometre hike for a sixtieth birthday, and is later accompanied by his own son on a trek around Mount Annapurna. 'Son following father and father following son.'

Norvig's argument is unwound in a lavishly illustrated book that is a pleasure to handle. Renchi invites her to don the blue robe and become 'Interpreter' for his quest. Just as Samuel Palmer and his youthful Ancients named William Blake in his straitened but resilient old age in Fountain Court. Norvig points out that in Plate 12 of Blake's *Pilgrim's Progress* sequence, Interpreter 'holds the key' to the complexity of the dream labyrinth.

Plate 2, *Christian Reading in His Book*, depicts a muscular, stooped figure burdened by a carapace rucksack, heavy head in an open volume. Against a backdrop of walled city and jagged mountain peak. This image, in full colour in *Dark Figures in the Desired Country*, was emblematic for me. Christian is plodding, as I read it, at sunset, from left to right of frame, west to east. Out beyond the walls of the established city, into the wastelands. He is loaded like a prospector's mule. Or like poor John Clare, heading across flat country to Boston in Lincolnshire, with a sack of his own remaindered books on his back. Or like so many schleps I undertook, with cumbersome stock rescued from the street markets of London.

Christian Reading in His Book was the only possible frontispiece for *Lud Heat*, my account of a period labouring in riverside places, under the shadow of the Hawksmoor churches. 'The man could look no way but downwards.'

More recently, in the 2014 exhibition, *William Blake: Apprentice & Master*, at the Ashmolean in Oxford, my eye was caught by Blake's watercolour *John Bunyan Dreams a Dream*. Sleeping on the ground, dos-à-dos with a cuddly lion, the exhausted pilgrim is the model for the sepulchral figure, dressed in lichen, on the monument plinth in the non-conformist burial ground at Bunhill Fields. A posthumous dream spills in a curve of progressed incidents across the horizon. And there, once again, is the bowed figure departing the city, burden on back, limping towards enlightenment.

The three life-walks of Renchi's recapitulation of *A Pilgrim's Progress* confirmed my instinct to return to Gower. The difference being that my triptych of hikes over the wave-cut Carboniferous limestone pavements covered the

same ground. I have to repeat: *place is poem.* No longer or more demanding road was required. Once, at seventeen, in hormonal confusion, relishing the atmosphere. Next, as a mature initiation, with Catling, reading and measuring, and making the rock spine the armature for years of work. And, again, at seventy-one, with Anna beside me: ground as memory, as resolution. As nothing but itself.

What I recover from the journal extract for January 4, 1973, found in the catalogue sheets of the *Albion Island Vortex* show at the Whitechapel Gallery, beyond the over-excited prose of that period, is the sense of transition between sitting in a car, heavy with London thoughts and conversations, and stepping out to begin the walk.

The car is parked in the corner of a sea field and the first salt sensations are transmitted through a curved filter, a wing of road greases. Motorway space is compressed and contained within this metal thorax.

As the door opens, held density spills.

A slate-stained morning, no violence. Distance sprung on a weighted immediacy: seabirds, insects, tufted grass. A grey ocean generating the pulse of buried earth motors.

The stereoscopic abruptness of this vision skins the eye, peeling road dirt from the cones and rods. An arc of bloodlight pushes at the pearly horizon. All noises, fumes, aches, anxieties are left in the vehicle. All the blocked intestinal brickdust of city labyrinths. The headclamp is still on, walking will break it. This Gower path, unknown and misremembered, is active; a weapon against the inertia of London life.

Light is compressed within the spine. It enters without retinal censorship. Crouched landforms. Inhaled silence.

The track ahead pushes a narrow tunnel through the bracken. It is a fact that confounds us, a dream rib. The drift of our movement is early and unmarked. But this is not a dream of revamped personal histories and we do not claim it. There is a surge of recognition, we are entering

the corridor of archetypes. All these stones have their form and extension from the ground of that primal dream in which we are choking, buried alive, throats clogged with earth. We breathe death. We claw out from it. Behind every faltering step we take is the huge limestone motive; mass that has not been worn and polished by a mere traffic of feet, nor stamped into a set of stone mirrors. The marine necropolis beyond Port Eynon Point swallows light, giving nothing back.

The path turns from the lazy contours of the dune line, a nuisance of thorn and thistle, and sharply towards evidence of the actions of ice, wind, water. A steep moment. Scale is unreadable. The domesticated eye forfeits its credibility. Embarked, there is no alternative. The giant slowness of the landscape gives the mind space to release the kite. The camera is lifted. Saline coating on the blue bulge of the lens. The shutter blinks to register grey fornications of rock and light. An oblique grammar is laid out in this ground: fungoid growths, mounds, cliff profiles, interconnected bone-caves.

At this point the true walk begins: stone-glare scalds the emulsion from our nerve plates. The rocks are dreaming us, translating impulse into image, speaking with tongues.

On the headland, in the wind, we hear the haunted sound of a sea bell, like the echo of a drowned cathedral. And I remember Vernon Watkins. 'With a quoit of stone he startled the bells / That sleep in the rocks' vibrating core.'

The narrative of that 1973 walk can only be resurrected from a negotiation between an unsorted heap of black-and-white photographs, in which established geographical features appear in the wrong order, as if we were constantly doubling back on ourselves, and full-colour stabs of memory: scents, scrambles, bruises, points of vantage with the craggy

headlands lined up like museum horses at the start of a race.

You might imagine, from the evidence of the photographs, that the walk was all rock. Catling plays the last man on earth, or an unfortunate time-traveller catapulted into the Pleistocene. He hooks himself to the cliff face, musing on vanished grass and the total absence of plant or animal life. He could have crashed on an alien planet, or subsided into a J.G. Ballard pumice-desert brought about by climate change. Later, recovering his spirits, he plods up barren slopes between Dalí outcrops and neural peaks. He wears a pouch of provisions on a strap across his chest, like a Cretan guerrilla searching for the right cave.

We never find it. Goat's Hole, Paviland. The Red Lady. She was part of my evolving Welsh myth of origin, but I had yet to make her acquaintance, even though my visit to Swansea Museum confirmed the fact that she was journeying under the wrong sexual passport. The bones, thought to be 26,000 years old, were still earth-red, but brittle, exposed, *dumped*. Flinging them in a glass coffin was a staging post to the incinerator.

There are other crevices, other holes to explore. We are slanting west, following the sun. Between Overton Cliff and Blackhole Gut, we are absorbed in making a record of the stones, in scrambling down to the shoreline and back to the path. Catling's rapid sketches will become ink drawings, closely related to the kind of large-scale sculptures he was attempting at that period; environments with wood, leather, steel and bone that became chambers within rooms.

After three or four miles, all knowledge of what has been left behind fades. The cliff path, rising and falling, has an inevitability that we begin to associate with patterns of migration; small groups, clad in animal skins, edging between a wooded interior and the steep drop to a plain running away to a remote sea. Investigating mounds, shallow declivities, supposed Iron Age forts, Bronze Age burial cairns, and off to the right, skeletal patterns of medieval field systems, carries us above and beyond the slade that offers a traverse to the Upper Palaeolithic burial in Paviland. We miss the essential site, but that does not invalidate the day's walk. Sometimes it works best to keep the desired conclusion in play. To know when it has to be left for another time. For now, we settle for an unexplained crown of burnt bush, looking like fused barbed wire.

By early afternoon, the way opens into grassland, thin soil stained with yellow splashes. Looking back, you are treated to a run of jutting headlands, emphasised by an angry white rim of water, waves breaking in clouds of foam on black rocks. Things grow, if you take the trouble to notice them, in cracks and faults, on ledges where seabirds perch and crap. Mary E. Gillham, in *The Natural History of Gower*, published in 1977, tells us that 'Gower's special plants seem to be a relic from Pre-Boreal and Boreal times just after the Ice Age.' They have crossed the land bridge from Europe, 'probably travelling through the developing forests along the rocky ridges of old moraines.' Fungal clusters belong in another time. Mushrooms with collagen lips are in multiple occupation of a few inches of cracked stone. Spleenworts in active possession of cave walls. Yellow lichens and blood-red wounds flush ecstatically in the exposed strata of Old Red Sandstone at the cliff base.

Before we passed beyond Mewslade Bay and reached the exposed neck of Worm's Head promontory, we made a couple of images as demonstrations of our quite distinct responses to this walk. Catling, in foetal ball, mimicked ritual burial among the shells and shards of a grassy hollow. Head tucked against knees. Hands folded into fingerless clumps. Mudded boots. Black clothes. With one disconcerting detail: several inches of exposed white cuff set off with heavy square links. While I, in silhouette, fists dangling, squat at the entrance of a cave I have no memory of visiting, above the glistening limestone pavement, at the sea's edge.

As Catling says in *The Vorrh*: 'We are dissolved . . . Such is the price of all trespass: Clever men and dolts give it up with joy; others struggle and claw against it, burning their hand bones to hooks, until fatigued or abased to nothing.'

One of the discoveries I made when searching for the *Albion Island Vortex* catalogue was a set of slithery pages held together with staples from the period of the 1973 Gower walk: faded poems, a text that the author, Brian Catling, had forgotten. The handwritten title was *The Vorrh*.

CERI RICHARDS AND
BLACK APPLE OF GOWER

R ed bones in the cave. Black apples buried deep in the rock.
Drowned bells sounding the headland. Wherever the key
to the essential mystery of the 'island' of Gower lies, it reveals
itself through symbols exposed and tested in the poetry of

Vernon Watkins and the paintings of Ceri Richards. Two quiet,
determined men; good neighbours at Pennard. Watkins in his
family bungalow. And the London-based Richards, who grew
up in neighbouring Dunvant, in his holiday home. They met
and were immediate friends – and, very soon, collaborators.
Ceri's wife, Frances, a ceramicist and a late poet, remembers:

'Ceri was immensely impressed with Vernon's appearance. His elegant figure and beautiful white hair that floated in the breeze as he strode along the coast to see us was a delight . . . The two men were both lovely to look at and fascinating to listen to; the friendship of Vernon and Ceri was very dear and sweet to me.'

One aspect of the relationship between poet and painter, consummated in Gower, can be ascertained in the responses they made, on their own terms, to the over-rehearsed and all too sudden death of Dylan Thomas. They did not succumb to pastiche or illustration. They identified parallel tracks through territory Thomas had opened up. It is known that Ceri Richards, on November 7 and 8, 1953, completed a series of loose-wristed, lyrical drawings in his copy of *Collected Poems (1934 – 1952)*. Thomas died, hours later, on November 9. Eighteen years, to the day, before Richards.

When I visited Rhiannon, the younger daughter of the painter, at her home in Barnes, she told me that her father undertook the project as a conscious charm against approaching darkness. Richards was aware of the reluctance to travel and the need for it that Dylan manifested on the only occasion they met, at the Boathouse in Laugharne, shortly before the troubled poet left for the USA. He flew out from Heathrow with three copies of the *Under Milk Wood* script made by the BBC producer Douglas Cleverdon: after Dylan, sweating and trembling, had tried so hard to lose the original in Soho. As if, in getting rid of this terrible thing, he could unpick the Faustian contract.

There is no cure for genius. The charm doesn't take in the way Ceri hoped. The painter had an implicit trust in the cycles of nature: death, decay, renewal. Eros and thanatos.

Blossom, ash. The hollow eye sockets of skulls flowering in midwinter spring. Scroll and shroud. Lovingly defaced first editions of *Collected Poems* were presented to Ceri's wife, his sister and a patron. With another copy, purchased from the artist, finding its way, as the poet Richard Burns reveals in *Ceri Richards and Dylan Thomas: Keys to Transformation* (1981), to the reserve collection in Swansea Central Library.

The drawings Richards undertook, in a state of fugue, in the margins and white spaces of the Thomas book, operated as a seance-communication with a poet sinking into his final coma, insult to the brain, and letting it all go among the ancestral voices, the fires of beginning. The London drawings exploited many of the same devices Dylan was dredging up with such mortal strain, in his last days in the 24-hour city, for the ghost play of *Under Milk Wood*. Richards would enhance the Folio Society version published in 1972. And, on that occasion, his drawings, charming and true to source, *are* illustrations. They give form and human warmth to the unseen presences of the night-masque. Here was the great dreamwork tourist text for which Wales was waiting. Jobs for all the famous faces forever. Singers, actors, comedians. Drunks. *To begin at the beginning. . .* And to end, or leave off, with the spring awakening in the second dark.

The hands of the artist, sketched like atavistic prints from a cave wall, hold the script open. The painter is a writer and the writer a painter; nibs scratch, words flower and choke. Stanzas melt into calligraphic seascapes. Black ink spurts. Much of the work is scene-setting for a Thomas performance that never happened, for which Richards was commissioned to provide the dropcloths: seahorses, spiralling suns, naked lovers. Then there are pages making specific reference to place. And pages where Richards takes the Gower theme, the mythology of the black apple and the cave, beyond the prompting of the fixed text. The title page and the page with the dedication – 'To Caitlin' – are a record of the recent visit to Laugharne. Dylan on the balcony of the Boathouse under gathering clouds. Caitlin, arms folded, unsmiling, beside the estuary. An abandoned lunch table laid out with bottles and no food.

'Milled dust of the apple tree and the pounded islands . . . Apple seed glides.' Herons. Hawks. Candles. Covered faces and closed eyes.

Beneath the nine lines of the poem 'Twenty-four years', Richards props the curly-headed poet beside a Vernon Watkins cliff in Gower. One hand on hip, while the other scratches his head. 'In the groin of the natural doorway I crouched.'

Ceri Richards, in the burn of inspiration, emphasised local mysteries layered into the dark measures of the verse. And he encrypted further mysteries of his own. Stock symbols refer us back to privileged viewpoints. And 'natural doorways' reference caves, explored or not yet visited. Dismembered fingers point at maps we do not possess. The Egyptian geometry, pyramid and inverted pyramid, of the poet's metaphysical sequence, 'Vision and Prayer', is duplicated in a Richards maze, under a cone of falling stars.

The key transformative image, as Richard Burns points out, is located in Ceri's response to the poem 'I dreamed my genesis'. He is left with most of a blank page on which to work, beneath the last four lines. 'I dreamed my genesis in

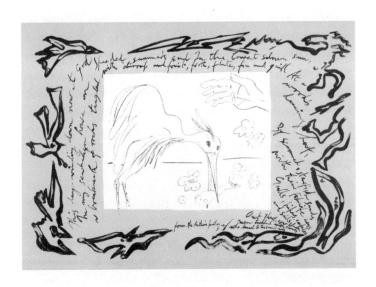

sweat of death. . .' Craggy Gower cliffs, such as are seen at Pennard, looking towards Pwlldu Head, or from Paviland back to Port Eynon Point, are presented under shell-pattern clouds. An owl and other creatures of the dream are hidden within the elemental mass of the cliff, crawling or flying or staring right through us. But the design is weighted around a nimbus of darkness that can be interpreted as spinning inwards, an exposed cavern, or rising hungrily towards the viewer. This is *Afal du Brogwyr*, the 'Black Apple of Gower'.

The integrity of the black apple, this opiate lump of *nigredo*, is unnerving. It's a war shield with La Tène Celtic embellishments, bellying towards the eye. And the shield of some implacable machine boring down into the rock. The decorations are sexual, suspended between fixed identities, male and female, testis and ovary. Night-seeds in a limestone pod. Burns suggests that the Gower cliffs enclosing the black apple 'could be interpreted as a partially developed vision of the paradisal island of Ys or Avalon'. *Partially developed.* A circular photographic plate swimming in a dish of chemicals. Or the cyclopean lens of a camera obscura catching beams from Glastonbury Tor, on the other side of the Bristol Channel.

The Isle of Apples. The fortunate isle. Sacred light from the Somerset levels – with abbey, spine of hill, thorn tree, spiral paths and stump of tower – balancing the alchemical darkness of the cliffs and caves across the water in Wales.

There were other 'Black Apple' versions too: paintings, line drawings. And a watercolour, a chalk on wood 'Mandala', presented to Carl Jung. Jung responded to this gift from Mrs Lucille Frost, friend and patron of Richards, by writing to the

I dreamed my genesis in sweat of death, fallen
Twice in the feeding sea, grown
Stale of Adam's brine until, vision
Of new man strength, I seek the sun.

painter. 'The round thing is one of many. It is astonishingly filled with compressed corruption, abomination and explosiveness . . . I understand your picture as a confession of the secret power of our time.' Richards replied: 'The circular image . . . is the metaphor expressing the sombre germinating force of nature – surrounded by the petals of a flower and seated within earth and sea.'

The physical force of the artist's hand makes that circle bite into paper. Keeping the pregnancy of the black womb, replete with its coils and curves, embryos and bitter fruits, distinct from the geological cross-section of Gower Peninsula and the crenellation of surrounding sea. 'Motor muscle on the drill,' Dylan Thomas wrote. Summoning a Vorticist response from an artist who had proved himself adept at making relief constructions with wood and plaster; paintings that were also sculptures. 'I dreamed my genesis', the poem from 1934 that fired Richards, forged a *nigredo* of its own in a phrase calling up the coming obscenity of European genocide: 'Death on the mouth that ate the gas.'

The motive thrust of that black apple scorched another, very different poet too: Geoffrey Hill. On the far side of Offa's Dyke, Hill registered 'the charring of permafrost / Or the sun's giving up the ghost / Of its corona'. He was lifted and caught in the cramp of the complexities of his lately discovered relationship with Wales, as he paid out the tight skein in *Oraclau/Oracles* (2010). In an interview published in *Poetry Wales* (Summer 2010), Hill says: 'It was almost as though I had spent my life wanting to be forgiven and accepted, and it seemed that in some miraculous way, at the age of seventy-one or seventy-two, I had been forgiven and accepted.' My own instinct, at the same age and with something of the same confusion, was the confirmation that I was not accepted. And nothing was forgiven. A landscape it was perfectly acceptable to flatter with sentiment had no use for my blind stumblings. Hill's cruel eye, with its forensic analysis of the seed on the slide, honoured process. The distance, in blood and pulse from Ceri Richards, was an advantage. 'The black mandala out of Wales,' he wrote, 'with anthrax in its seams.' 'Introfusion of vision: / Poetry of such corruption and fire / Baking the lily in its dung.' He purges the mysteries of the Black Sun. 'Not everything is rotten in Carl Jung.'

Ceri Richards was born on June 6, 1903, in Dunvant, a mining village on the western edge of Swansea, near the start of the inland road to the Gower Peninsula. He grew up in the orthodoxy of chapel and music and close family. When the time came, he got away to London, on a scholarship to the Royal College of Art. And he stayed. He married a talented fellow student, Frances Clayton of Burslem in the Potteries. They had two daughters and lived for the rest of their lives, apart from a wartime stay in Cardiff, in London: Chelsea, Hammersmith, Wandsworth. There was also the holiday house at Pennard, where Richards, before he started his day's work, took out a pair of binoculars to watch the ritual of Vernon Watkins scampering for the bus.

I came across Richards' work for the first time as a schoolboy in Cheltenham; large-scale swirling complexities, if I remember them right, perhaps *Cycle of Nature* or one of the series made after Delacroix, in a group exhibition. The singing colour, the trace elements of a molten, pantheistic surrealism, registered. A painterly verve against so much that struck me as arid and restrained. *And English*. Richards, I subsequently discovered, was an early encourager of Francis Bacon. Homeric beasts metamorphose into columns of grapes and red eyes and supple organs of generation.

The first artwork I purchased, and it is still with me, was the Ceri Richards lithograph, 'Do not go gentle into that good night', from the Dylan Thomas poem. I saw it in an exhibition at the Howard Roberts Gallery in Cardiff, while

I was still trying to make something more of the poet than I'd been able to do in the rush of that school project. Now, leaving Wales for London, this black-and-white image, savage and rhetorical, travelled with me as a permanent backdrop, the perfectly realised metaphor for the futility of writing. And the inevitability. The naked poet forked and splayed on the curve of a stage reminiscent of one of those Francis Bacon sets. The owl bearing away shroud-sheets fouled with words. Circle of brilliant moon as a hole punched in the black sky. Shading on poet's body like dirty thumbprints. Hands and feet prehensile, spaghetti-stretched like those of a man sucked into the impossible density of a black hole singularity. Eyes and teeth bared in Picasso rictus.

My wife never liked the picture. But tolerated, without serious complaint, its presence in all the rooms and houses where we lived over the next fifty years. Darkness within and without. When the lithograph is turned on its head, the body of the fallen man becomes another topographic study: Gower's rocky rim, with inlets, coves, headlands. And the owl, whose face stares with the same ferocity whichever way up you take it, is the votive creature hidden in the strata of the 'Black Apple' drawing. The moon is the apple printed in reverse, a bulb of pure chalk.

In Peterborough, on one of the infrequent book-searching expeditions when Anna accompanied me, in the promise of a detour to Glinton, the home village of her father's family, we followed up on the rumour of a dealer who had a set of drawings of John Clare on his foot-foundered 'Journey out of Essex'. They were by Rigby Graham, an artist closely associated with Mike Goldmark, the publisher of my first novel, who had now opened a gallery in Uppingham. I'd seen some of Rigby's lithographs of Clare; including one of an owl who might have flown straight from the signboard of the Lippitts Hill pub, close to Matthew Allen's asylum, and on to sagging telegraph wires above the embattled figure of the Helpston poet in the battered top hat, as he strikes off on the long road.

I looked through the sequence of Graham drawings. They made Clare's progress flicker like a silent film through landmarks adjudicated by the Leicestershire artist on his reprise of a journey, Epping Forest to the fenland rim, that was now turning into an English rite. The painful silence of the solitary walker seeds off-highway corridors with acoustic bands of poetry. Future tramps find phrases locking into their heads. 'Life to me a dream that never wakes.' Lengthening shadows of absent pilgrims. 'A frost-bound thought that freezes life to stone.'

There was a framed picture on the Peterborough wall, executed with a freedom of line reminiscent of Matisse; elements pared down, so that there was just enough in the rectangle to let the composition breathe without making it appear undernourished. An unnumbered artist's proof, so we were told, by Ceri Richards. His response to 'Poem in October' by Dylan Thomas. A blue and yellow vision of 'the heron priested shore'.

In the empty space at the bottom of the page in the copy of *Collected Poems* that Richards illuminated, he drew a sunflower-sun touching the sea above crosshatched headlands. The artist injected the missing colour from those pen-and-ink sketches into this Peterborough exhibit; solar flares were crayoned around the rim. A heron on stalk legs, a fish in its beak. A blue river with oxbow curves. And the naked fallen man from my 'Do not go gentle' lithograph. He has not yet reached the ground. He is headless, neck cropped at the picture's rim. This figure is overlaid with a slate-grey miasma, dotted like cave art.

Anna is entranced. We go away, discuss it, and are in agreement. We return for a second viewing. We make a purchase we can barely afford, sharing the cost. The lightness of touch, the open spaces, the blues and yellows Richards employs in his lyrical rendering of the Vernon Watkins poem 'Music of Colours: White Blossom' confirm this picture as the necessary household balance to its dark counterpoint, that interior journey with owl and shroud. If my earlier purchase belongs in a working space among books and stones, this one with its river of life, bird and fish has to be lodged in the kitchen.

Living on everyday terms with this image in the place where we ate, talked, made coffee, read newspapers, watched squirrels headbutt the window and rank foxes scatter chicken bones and burger cartons, produced a casual intimacy. The Richards lithograph was a portal into remembered places, the blue river a baptism that could go horribly wrong. 'Summertime of the dead.'

I acquired Richards catalogues. We travelled to Cardiff for the major retrospective at the National Museum and Gallery of Wales in 2002. I bought and absorbed Mel Gooding's *Ceri Richards*, a painstaking and lavishly illustrated account of the Dunvant artist's life and career. Gower, as source of inspiration, was a dominant presence. Gooding's double-page photograph, used for the endpapers, was of those wave-cut Carboniferous limestone pavements, with a yellow thread of coast path. I noticed how herons, rivers, owls, skulls stuffed with flowers, were resident motifs. Particularly where Richards was channelling Dylan Thomas, or charting the terrestrial and supernal mythologies of Gower.

A crayon-and-pastel drawing from 1964, *Homage to Dylan Thomas*, has the freedom of our kitchen lithograph. A heron to the left of the river, fish in beak. Waxy darts of yellow. Shroud-owl in place of the fallen poet. The penultimate Richards drawing, in his copy of *Collected Poems*, moves the heron to the other side of the Taf estuary, so that it is now looking back, east, from Laugharne towards Gower. In the 'Swansea' version, the title *Collected Poems* is outlined to become the fish in the heron's beak.

I began to appreciate, digging a little deeper, how securely the landscape of the painter's obsession is anchored in Pennard, not abstractions derived from his interest in Max Ernst and Surrealism, or grafts factored from his close reading of poetry. Mel Gooding, in his account of the friendship between Ceri Richards and Vernon Watkins, speaks of the way the poet led the painter to 'personal vantage points' – as if presenting him with special views that had to be recovered and represented. Watkins, Gooding says, 'was remarkably sure-footed. Far down on the foreshore, when you came to see him, and the tide was right – you saw him from aloft – and he was master with the prawns, crabs and lobsters, striding through pools, over rocks slippery with seaweed, up rocky faces and sand dunes, and through acres of bracken and gorse, in his own natural diversity of ways.' Speed of movement is the acknowledgement that there is more to be

touched on than time and fading light allow. In his poem of place, 'Taliesin in Gower', Watkins puts his own creed into the mouth of his elective predecessor: 'I witness here in a vision the landscape to which I was born.'

Paintings by Richards from the '40s, like *Welsh Landscape* and *Welsh Coast*, as well as earlier pieces using *frottage*, rubbings of the grain in wood, fix the zone between cliff and beach in which improvisations from the poetry of Dylan Thomas and Vernon Watkins will manifest. Paint is dragged across canvas, sweeping strokes mimicking rock strata in a liquid state. 'The organism decomposes,' Gooding writes, 'and returns to its mineral matrix.' It is a challenge to know if the works came before the places they invoked. We have to discover for ourselves if walking and re-walking nominated paths can break down that distinction.

As an epigram for his book *The Whispering Swarm*, Michael Moorcock quotes a provocative notion from Tarkovsky. The idea that those we see as alien, travellers from remote solar systems, are in fact our common ancestors, adrift in whirlpools of time, and arriving here to confront us. 'That is our future'. To meet the parts of ourselves that journey out from the caves and bone pits and cromlechs, fighting to stay ahead of the advance of ice.

The lyre birds came from Jersey. On one of my book-buying trips, I was offered a box, with a lyre bird design on the cover, containing a number of ink-and-gouache drawings produced by Ceri Richards in response to an invitation from Tambimuttu, the editor of the magazine *Poetry London*. They were executed in 1943, the year of my birth, in Cardiff, where Richards had been appointed Head of Painting at the Art School. The box came from the estate of Colin Anderson, a notable supporter of Ceri and his family. In 1939, at a time when money was tight, Anderson arranged for Ceri and Frances to take a house in the village of Alphamstone, on the Suffolk/Essex border, at a token rent.

Richards enjoyed making gifts of drawings tipped-in to treasured books, often poetry, or watercolours, such as the lyre birds which were never published by Tambimuttu.

He wrote to Colin Anderson from Bishops Road in Cardiff in December 1943. 'Frances and I are sending you some lyre birds for your Christmas fare and we hope they are to your taste ... These few are just a good choice from the very many that are scattered about.'

The commission for the birds came to its crisis. The never reliable Tambi, tapping for funds, soliciting work he would never be able to use, in pubs and drinking dens, bookshops, private houses, had a gift for brokering fortuitous connections. Asking, for example, Graham Sutherland to provide the imagery that binds David Gascoyne's *Poems 1937 – 1942* for Editions: Poetry London. And nudging Ceri Richards towards Dylan Thomas. Sutherland and Richards, in wartime, were drawing on some of the same sources: Picasso, Ernst, Welsh landscape. Comets, moons, caves, fires. The codes of poetry were closer to the surface then. The impulse I felt, making Gower walks, was now a command: use the gravity of place as a technique for psychic alignment with earlier attempts to interrogate structures that defy communication. By arranging and rearranging groups of fixed symbols. In Cardiff in 1943, Ceri, patrolling warehouse roofs, was a firewatcher.

Issue No. 11 of *Poetry London* appeared in September 1947 with a Henry Moore lyre bird on the cover. Inside was a double-page spread of lithographed illustrations by Ceri Richards, text in the artist's holograph: 'The force that through the green fuse drives the flower'. And so begins the intimate engagement with Dylan Thomas. The lyre bird series can be read as preliminary exercises on the same theme. Hand-lettered words. Preening feathers becoming musical instruments. The materials of song and poetry held apart, as yet, from identification with place.

I kept one of the drawings and presented it to Anna. Two birds. The pink – male? – puffed up, an erected fan of feathers as lyre. The blue-grey female looking away. That's how I interpret it. The rest of the box, with the letter from Richards to his patron, went into auction. The money realised, along with what I raised by selling off a substantial chunk of the collection of Beat books by Burroughs, Kerouac and others that I'd accumulated over the years, gave me the funds to write my first novel. I hadn't published anything of substance in eight years, as I slogged around the country excavating stock for my bookstall in Islington. The Richards lyre birds arrived just when they were needed, before the material I was cooking, so slowly, went from chilled to dead in the mouth. Stranger still, as I discovered years later, the successful bidder for the Richards box was Mike Goldmark, the man who published my book. One of the lyre birds, nicely framed, now hangs in his house.

On January 14, 2015, I took the London Overground from Haggerston to Clapham Junction, where I changed to make the connection to Barnes. It was a morning with plenty of sparkle in the light, scouring the dirty windows of the enclosed walkway above that promiscuous spill of track. It felt right to buy a bunch of bright yellow roses to carry with me to the house of Rhiannon, the second daughter of Ceri and Frances Richards, on the anniversary of my own second daughter's birth. Rhiannon was married to Mel Gooding, who had curated a number of Richards shows, as well as writing the definitive account of his life and work. Mel offered me the chance to look at some of the key items for my Gower project, including the first copy of the Dylan Thomas *Collected Poems* with the artist's drawings.

The house was tucked away in a quiet street, not far from Barnes Common. Builders were in evidence, this was a recent move. We settled at a long table for a hospitable lunch of pasta and wine. This convivial space, alongside the cooking area, was open to garden and screened railway. Paintings glowed on every wall. The kitchen was *alive*. With bright plates on Welsh dresser. And items of rescued farmhouse furniture, for use not decoration. The roses were the right colour, at home with other yellows and companionable blues. Paintings were not all by Ceri Richards. There were large confident pieces by Gillian Ayres and Terry Frost. Upstairs, among the books, was a neurotically brilliant Fred Janes pineapple that invoked Arcimboldo by way of Magritte. Janes, at one time, had a rambling Gower farmhouse, not far from Pennard. He was the one who took Ceri Richards to meet Dylan Thomas.

It did feel as if I was impinging on a series of personal contacts and affinities that tied together a London-Welsh set of independent and very different artists: Fred Janes, Ceri Richards, David Jones in his Harrow trench. All of them had some engagement with Vernon Watkins. Anecdotes followed. Warm memories were exchanged. Coincidences. Epiphanies. Quotations.

Gooding lent me *Requiem and Celebration*, a book of poems by a friend, another Dunvant man, John Ormond. Ormond made films on Dylan Thomas, Ceri Richards and Vernon Watkins. The poem that caught my eye was 'My Grandfather and His Apple-Tree'. 'All light was beckoning.' A farm boy goes beneath ground into the coal measures. Returned to the surface, he limes an apple tree and makes it sweet, but that sweetness is 'budded temptation in his mouth'. He grafts the sourness of a cooking apple. The final image in the poem spikes something I remember from childhood, an old gardener 'grinding thin slices that his jack-knife cut'. He sucks juice from the rind and spits into a spread of nettles. The offer of peeled fruit, and its sharp clean taste, rescued me when I left home, aged seven, for the school in Porthcawl. And when I realised, definitively, that there was no going back, I had wandered out into the walled garden where they grew the vegetables they boiled to death, along with fruit bushes and a few scrawny apple trees.

Rhiannon saluted the stories of Dylan Thomas and the lost paradise of childhood. She spoke about her father decorating the white spaces of *Collected Poems* as a charm against dying. The holiday home in Pennard had gone. New people, successful business folk, were pouring out of Swansea, knocking down the bungalows, putting up breezeblock walls and box-buildings with picture windows.

Mel remembered Ceri's father, Tom Richards, the Dunvant tinplate worker; and how, on a hot summer walk, he wouldn't step inside a pub, even to partake of lemonade. The rigour of non-conformist faith. All this was familiar too. Richards was the family name of my mother's mother. The whole tribe were chapelgoers coming east from Carmarthen and Cardigan. My grandmother's brother was another Tom Richards. There were plenty around. I grew up drifting in and out of their bilingual kitchen stories. Corpse candles. Deaths foretold. Ghost paths. Mari Llwyd. Walks over the hills to Neath Fair. And an old aunt, swathed in layers of bombazine black, who swam every day from Llanstephan to Ferryside, across the mouth of the Towy.

We went upstairs. Mel had laid out the Ceri Richards sketches and the books that made reference to Gower. There were large ink drawings of inland panoramas, ridges, cliff spreads. Topographic records, energetic and free-flowing, but innocent of the system of coded symbols: no owls, no apples. No Goat's Hole Cave.

It was fascinating to see how Richards worked so directly to make drawings in books that were confirmations of what he already knew: not so much collaboration as possession by the same spirits that shook and destroyed the poets. Dark angels, charged by storms local to Gower, whispered their heresies. The drawings were language before words. Colours had their sounds. Yellows and blues were favoured for priestly herons. Mel showed me a sketch of bird, fish, river, from June 1971, the year of Ceri's death. 'High tide and the heron dived when I took the road.' Birthday poems choked on sticky pollen hooks, dust of plant-fractured rock, sunspots dancing on water. Charms against whatever was clenched and folded in the womb of the buried apple.

On one of the blank preliminary pages in *Fidelities* by Vernon Watkins, published by Faber in 1968, shortly after the poet died in Seattle, Richards made a pencil and crayon drawing, blues and yellows again, that reprised the elements we looked at every day in the 'Poem on his birthday' lithograph. Once again the spindly heron, beak wedged with god-fish, presides over the blue, baptismal river: all the Old Testament yowls of Methodist elders in their hard chapel pews chorus approval. But now, for the first time, I am aware of the motif

being laid out against a Gower backdrop, a schematic sweep of the cliffs at Pennard, looking west towards Port Eynon Point. The golden cross of the solar god high above the headland tells us where to launch the next walk. The sun is the atomic kernel of the apple. Wedding blossom drifts from the Watkins poem Richards loved, 'Music of Colours'. A sleeping horse reminds us of the wild ponies found on the high ground, the spine running through Gower, with the shallow declivity and the scatter of rocks around the burial chamber known as 'Arthur's Stone'. 'We were transfigured,' Watkins wrote, ' by the deaths of others.'

There was also a painting returned as too blatant by a

daughter-in-law, a leaf-form, ripe, in fruit, but too directly a vulva, placed within firmly outlined curves on the surface of a table. Within which we are shown an open drawer containing a green apple. The work was from 1968, Mel said. And its title was *The Origin of Life*.

On my way home, I detoured by Overground railway to the southern suburbs. The carriages were standing room only: steaming, humming with neurotic digital pulses and weary human meat competing for limited air. But the charge of what I had seen in Barnes kept me floating, and even grateful to be part of the necessary transit of the city. A friend had recently been given bad news and faced an operation later that week. It had all happened so fast that we couldn't absorb the gravity of what this meant before it was on us. And over us. The young man was shaken, as he would be, by the way that the known world can shift so dramatically on its axis, in one instant, leaving the victim of diagnosis, against which there is no appeal, high and dry.

A close colleague had flown straight down from Glasgow, to share a curry and a few beers with his mate. This helped. It was normality. We had a chance to sit together for a few moments while the curry was dished out and the daughter of the house scampered about, unconcerned, telling us how to behave. The thing I wanted to communicate, with no justification beyond what I needed to be true, was the force of positive energy in contemplation of the words and images in the Ceri Richards collection I had viewed that afternoon. I pulled out a reproduction of *Black Apple of Gower*, to try and explain the nucleus of power in that transformative embellishment to the Dylan Thomas poem. 'The sombre germinating force of nature.'

Fresh from medical probes and intrusive investigations in Guy's Hospital, my friend, who had been diagnosed with testicular cancer, looked closely at the impacted darkness of the circular sac held in the rocks. 'That's my scan,' he said.

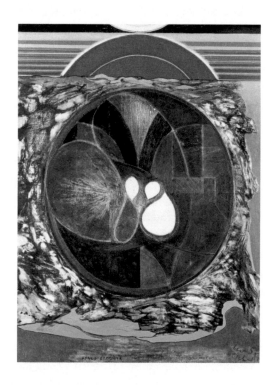

DROWNED CATHEDRAL

Arriving in Port Eynon with Anna, years after those other misremembered cliff walks, courtships and restorative escapes from London, here was an authentic return. A remaking for which the earlier attempts had been rehearsals. The morning of September 17, 2014, felt fresh and uncluttered. *And new.* This country had never been mine, but the persistent dream of it, a rather shop-soiled songline, held firm. Myths of origin underwrote our planned excursion by recently sanctioned coast path to Rhossili. Earlier auguries of trespass beyond the permissions of maps and charts had faded away. The contemporary Gower walk was burnished in weekend colour supplements, flagged up on websites, heralded in top-ten lists everywhere. Another bright-eyed old couple tottered from the car park, hiking poles at the ready, coshed by bracing salt air. We nodded in acknowledgement and exchanged Alpine salutes.

The monochrome of the Catling raid from 1973, that interplanetary adventure among the cairns and burial pits, was flooded with natural colour; subtleties of green and grey, ochre, sand, slate. The morning was ripe with honeysuckle, blackberries and butterflies. A jounce of approval for the better life in the springy ground. It felt as if a compulsory hiking app had been implanted in the spine, to replace the old sensation of climbing the first headland and having everything you thought you knew undone by daggered outcrops of rock, limestone pavements hammered from solidified smoke. Some form of remote and beneficent Kindle-control dictated the footsteps of obedient coast-path backpackers. We might all have been tied together on a length of rope. There was no deviation from the approved route. Pilgrims ticked off the shell of the Salt House, admired the lunar austerity of Sedgers Bank, and took out binoculars to collect appropriate seabirds. You could hear the slabs of Kendal Mint Cake clunking against reviving flasks of coffee. Tormentil and yellow lady's bedstraw dressed the pillows of gorse and ling that kept us insulated. And on track.

Anna had damaged her Achilles tendon, more through general wear and tear than any particular drama, and it was thought that she'd come along for a couple of miles to get the benefit of the day, then go back to bring the car round to Rhossili at some agreed time. But it was not yet decided how that time would be agreed, mobile phones were as useless as broken toys for communication among the stones.

Sea-sounds insinuated, invading the inner ear. The air was aniseed sweet. Anna's steady movements exposed an unspoken determination to complete the walk. She popped painkillers. She necked Red Bull. She sprayed, strapped. And strode out, driving her single, spiked pole into the sod. There were apples in her rucksack, along with water, plasters and talcum powder.

It was a gentle first ascent. The walk was a narrative

suitable for all grades of hiker and recreationalist. Hart's-tongue ferns, leathery green fronds. A scalp-raking thorn tunnel with a pewter path making the climb a green plunge

into an Ivon Hitchens painting. And reminding me, yet again, why Graham Sutherland and Ceri Richards found sustenance in Welsh coastal landscapes; topographies where cairns, caves and burial mounds were absorbed and incorporated into hill farms, quarries, the rough grazing of headlands and estuary marshes. Managed enchantment. The tidying up of the route, the signs that keep walkers on a permitted path, took nothing away from the liberating rush of what was always there: the unreadable mass of place.

I don't have the words, the accepted technical terms, for the natural forms that surround me. So that the scree of a decommissioned quarry, mounds of flints and sharp, broken stones, is welcomed. We are comfortable when history is visible but set aside, when it can be safely romanced and used as a set. I saw these Port Eynon workings as the backdrop for a potential Cinecittà muscle-boy programmer, *Hercules Conquers Atlantis*. American TV-oater imports and local talent with borrowed Hollywood names hurling huge rocks, like medicine balls made of foam, and rescuing very experienced virgins in mail-order nighties from Moors and pirates and rubber monsters. The Welsh sky had that heavenly blue of Umbrian muralists, Old Testament saints in rocky landscapes; a blue that traded on contrast with the sun-dazzled whiteness of native hills.

I was shuffling a set of cultural cartoons, holding to the Gower path by seeing it as anything but what it actually was: a decent walk, ion-impregnated air, the sea on one side, fields and small farms on the other. We were heading west-by-northwest, in a straight line, climbing and descending, deciding when and where to come away from the sanctioned track.

Anna, with more justification, was reminded of Brittany; her childhood, family camping holidays among the standing stones, going for milk and water to isolated farms. The burden of memory has to be spilled before we can begin to appreciate what is there in front of us. Her recollections are of storms, sulks, sickness, withheld ice-creams, mechanical failures, breakdowns, rain. Journals kept, with all the siblings taking it in turns to voice their grievances. Great times never to be forgotten. Or forgiven. The landscape forgot them at once.

The walk overrides the walker. We are ambling, quietly, without pressure or urgency, in a conspiracy of affection. When I knew Anna first and brought her down to Wales, I wanted to show off my special places, in the way that Vernon Watkins scampered about Pennard with Ceri Richards, barely allowing him time to expose an adequate mental impression before bounding away to the next point of vantage. We set off on long tramps around the Maesteg hills – and, once, insanely overburdened in the style of Anna's childhood, with pots, pans, tins of stew, tents, sleeping bags, on an intended expedition to Glynneath and on into Central Wales. We forgot that every valley was an abandoned coalmine, a fouled river, an impenetrable thatch of lightless conifers with dead undergrowth. We discounted the midges. And woke to cows licking Anna's exhausted face. But there were kinder excursions, to secret bays of Gower, to the cliffs at Monknash, the sand dunes at Merthyr Mawr, and the wilder beaches of the far west. But never, until now, this walk. Another small chapter to add to a lengthening saga.

I thought of what Richard Burns wrote about how drawings by Ceri Richards contain 'lines of force'. I interpret this to mean that the rhetoric of the presented image, a record of painterly performance, often includes, as a secondary element, covert diagrams of movement. The works are 'about' the moment in which they are constructed, but they are also a form of territorial map, in a mode reminiscent of Australian Aboriginal art. Every painting is a device for remembering. It has an occulted as well as a public meaning. If such a thing is going to live with us, in gallery or private house, a significant exchange is required. We live by what we choose to own. Paintings of landscape become, with the passage of time, self-portraits. Of selves we come very slowly to know and fear. 'They have a function both formal and meaningful,' Burns says. 'They denote the paths and concentrations of energy currents.'

Coming across the first headland above Overton Mere, and carrying on, quietly, not breaking off to revisit Culver Hole, it became clear, with nothing said, that Anna was not going back to the car. The pain settled to an acceptable level as she walked. It was also clear that I wouldn't be undertaking any major detours: this was now a shared enterprise.

We listened to the mournful sound of the sea bell. From these cliffs, the villagers of Port Eynon gathered in January 1883 to watch crews from Oxwich and Rhossili struggle to reach the *S.S. Agnes Jack*, a Liverpool vessel carrying 600 tons of ore from Llanelli to Sardinia. Taking shelter, while waiting

for the flood tide, the *Agnes Jack* was caught in a tremendous storm and grounded on the rocks of Sedgers Bank (or Skysea), that limestone ridge we had explored on our first afternoon in Horton. Rockets failed in the high wind. Small boats trying to take off the crew were reduced to matchwood on the rocks. None of the sailors reached the shore. Their bodies, smashed, scraped raw, were recovered. The men were buried, their names on a monument, in the churchyard of St Cattwg at Port Eynon. One crew member's body never returned from the sea. Cattwg, I told Anna, was a variant of Cadoc or Cadog. He is supposed to have been the Abbot of Llancarfan, son of one of the lesser Welsh princelings (warrior bandits). The interest being that he gave his name to a number of churches in Cornwall and Brittany. So her sense of common ground was confirmed. There are effigies of Saint Cadoc at Belz, in the country of the menhirs, dolmens and Neolithic standing stones, where Anna camped on her family holidays.

More than anything else, the tolling of the sea bell invoked the great series of Ceri Richards paintings made from Gower themes in parallel with the 'black apple' mandalas. If the apples were caves of origin set within the landscape to process cycles of nature, *La Cathédrale engloutie* belonged to the sea. The paintings were about looking down, registering a fret-board made from the forms and textures of shoreline: rock pools, patterns of wave crump, flickers of shimmering light on the open water. Synaesthesia. Fluid compositions using the architecture of musical instruments to score the harmonies of paint. Slow depths and swift surfaces. Dark blue, black. Yellow and silver.

In 1957, so Mel Gooding tells us, Richards acquired a high-fidelity Dynatron record player for his Chelsea studio. He listened to Debussy's piano prelude, *La Cathédrale engloutie*. The sunken cathedral. Ys in Brittany. One of a number of legends of drowned churches, cities lost to sudden deluges, punished settlements. The theme was resonant. Richards had visited Suffolk that year, to collaborate with Lennox Berkeley on his opera *Ruth*. He designed costumes and stage sets for the Aldeburgh Festival production. And he was back again the following year to work on Benjamin Britten's *Noye's Flood* for a performance in Orford Church. He took time to investigate Dunwich and the story of the inundated township with its drowned churches, lost to storm surges in the thirteenth century. Again the painter looks down from above, from tangled woods, on a site of disappearance. On the voracious North Sea (or German Ocean). And again there is a link to Vernon Watkins, who published his set of translations from Heinrich Heine, *The North Sea*, with Faber in 1955. Poems open on the repeated motif of a red sun dropping into the 'silver-grey of the world': water as a mirror of upturned sky. Architectural forms emerge. 'Churches' domes and towers revealed themselves, / And, at last, clear as sunlight, a whole town.' Natural sounds – wind, scrape of tide, screeching gulls – promote a new programme of work for the painter. He is back in his Chelsea studio, Debussy prelude on turntable: stories of bells reverberating through cold depths, hallucinations of vanished things.

An elevated viewpoint marks out the discrete stages of a walk that honours place and subverts time. Vernon Watkins worked and reworked the sonnets that became *Elegy for the*

Latest Dead, remembrances of Dylan Thomas, published in *Botteghe Oscure* XIII (Rome 1954). 'Above this path, high on the cliff we stood . . .' The two young Swansea poets compete, throwing 'knife-edge' stones in the direction of the sea. 'He crouched, listening for the scream below.' On another occasion, while Watkins swims, Dylan sees the rocks turn into 'human brutes', wage-slaves in 'correct grey suits' wallowing like seals. The symbols used by Ceri Richards are present too: 'The heron stoops above the stream.' Cliff walks. Confessions. Intimate exchanges. Words thrown out: to 'dramatize the void'.

La Cathédrale engloutie paintings deploy techniques and motifs essential to the development of Ceri Richards as an artist and a major interpreter of place. Music. Pantheism. Deep-topography. Eros. Archetype. The earlier works from the 1930s, modelled, relief-sculpted with abstractions in wood, are referenced. A number of the more playful pieces in this series have brass bells, small wooden pianos, crosses, crabs. Other keyboards are vertical, as seen through clear water: morning preludes of drowned pianos. Shapes recalling the *Black Apple of Gower* are cross-sections of rounded columns from lost churches or palaces; submerged suns, ammonites, rose windows, mineral roundels. 'An inexhaustible proliferation of forms and configurations,' Gooding says. From the unknowable darkness of the deeps, where blue becomes black, to an aerial perspective on reefs and islets and barnacled ridges. Richards spoke to his friend John Ormond about the prelude that inspired him. 'I knew Debussy's music quite well, and this one particularly reminded me, I suppose, of the Gower.'

Repeated walks, in company, with family and friends, or

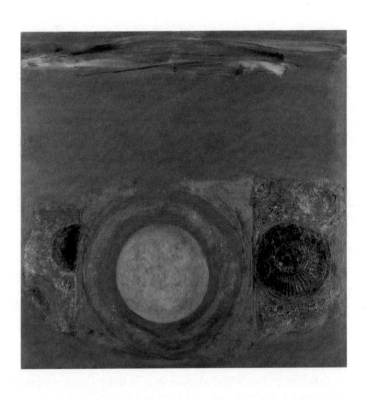

alone, over the same ground, drifting to the same viewpoints, watching the sun rise over Hunt's Bay or set over Oxwich, charge the painter with a powerful sense of obligation. He must develop an art that goes beyond what he knows and sees, but which is fed and sustained by recognition and recovery: the chimera of the past that is always out ahead. Decorative motifs from the late Iron Age filtered through close study of Picasso and the modernists. And fired by radar beacons of place. 'He brings to that sensory experience a visual imagination affected by a lifetime of wonder at the beauty of the Gower cliffs and rocky coastal shores,' Gooding wrote.

Anna's instinct was sound: Brittany, Gower. She remembered a visit to the Neolithic menhirs at Carnac. How the young children of the neighbourhood came rushing at her troop, hands out for coins, offering to 'explain' the stones. *Est ce-que je pourrais vous expliquer l'histoire de ces pierres?* The avenues. The alignments. They were probably laid out by ancient Bretons with a sense of humour, as a future theme park, an income generator. Carnac fishermen made a separate community. A resort grew up on the old salt flats. Gower fishermen were ghosts summoned by the sea bell. Poets and painters, haunting local heights, were overwhelmed by the voices of the returning drowned.

Visiting Anna's beloved fens, while researching a book on John Clare's 'Journey out of Essex', we came across a farm where carved stones from the quarries at Barnack, intended for Ely Cathedral, and lost from an overturned raft on Whittlesey Mere, rose up from the heavy ground. Cut. Marked. Ready to be slotted into place. Sunk in mud and sediment until the inland sea was drained. Sections of

a thirteenth-century cathedral suddenly appearing, breaking through the muck of a working farmyard: limestone blocks as golden as the day they were quarried.

That is how Ceri Richards envisioned the cathedral of Ys. Emerging from an alien element. Obedient to the laws of transformation. He looked down on the sea and charted, through paintings like a series of illuminated panel-windows, the ruins of the vanished island-city. The theme was as much Welsh as Breton. Richards invoked Cantre'r Gwaelod, the Neolithic settlement lost beneath Cardigan Bay; a folk memory kept alive in *The Black Book of Carmarthen*. Sonar traces, from a period when the sea between Wales and Ireland was rising, evolve into legends of chiming bells, heard at low tide on still evenings. 'The first light we have seen,' said the poet Robert Duncan, 'the incandescence of the dead.'

The path is well kept, single-file width; a safe step from the cliff's vertiginous edge. We encounter the other elderly excursionists from Port Eynon, wondering aloud if they should push on, or, as they eventually decide, turn back to the safety of the known, the car. But Anna is floating. Moving steadily forward, while I scramble off the track to investigate a set of recent stone circles and suspiciously geometric arrangements in the glacial debris beneath a pyramid peak with black slots and the shallow cave of Longhole. Greedy Victorians, in the material confidence of their period, denuded the site, removing a charmed memory-ballast in baskets heaped with the bones of cave bear, hyena, reindeer, lion, horse. The last mammoths went down around 12,000 years ago. Time slumbers, undisturbed, in the dark.

Scant turf is scratchy with gorse. Slades, like sexual invitations, winked and then withdrew. Narrow, steep-sided gorges cut by water running down to the glittering parenthesis of the green sea. And rock-cropped headlands where we pause to take the view. Gulls. Kittiwakes. Blackberry grenades to sweeten dry lips. One small tortoiseshell butterfly, in an orange-black feint of display, leads us on, welcomed as a modest ephemeral, where anything as showy on a human scale would be as loud as a *Coronation Street* landlady in high definition.

Veering closer to the road, and the village of Pilton Green, I realise that once again I've succeeded in missing the Goat's Hole Cave at Paviland. It's too late to make a traverse. Anna has done well on her damaged tendon, but the painkillers are beginning to wear off. The noisy cropping of sheep domesticates the approach to Mewslade Bay, drowning out that reverie of clanging sea bells. Their jeering bleat sounded very much like 'EEEE-an . . . Eeee-an . . . Iain.' A proper homecoming at last. In the cloudless Welsh sky, a knot of black feathers stamping thermals to hold a position above a tired or terminally bored hare. This furry creature, stretching its full length, ears erect, yawns. It gazes, unblinking and old-man-rheumy, out to sea.

The flattened skull of the Worm's Head promontory was cut off by the tide. I was a field or so ahead of Anna as we trespassed into an entirely new script. The official path, up against a dry-stone wall, from the village of Rhossili to the Worm's Head, called itself 'Gower Way'. But it felt like Hackney Wick, a gaudy procession to a warehouse rave. I thought I was hallucinating a touring production of *Miss Saigon*: Chinese girls in minimalist outfits spangled like golden gift-wrappings, Japanese couples chattering on multiple iPhones, while they digitally hoovered field and beach and Lookout Station. The new gimmick was a small camera fixed on a wand, so that intertwined lovers could star in their own movie.

Was this about Dylan Thomas? Air-con coaches with black windows, as for rock tours, debouched regiments of the unregimented, to hobble on unsuitable heels and dainty slippers towards the neck of rock, the stone-frozen dragon of Worm's Head. The scene reminded me of a recent excursion to Holy Island in Northumberland. There must be some buzz in the idea of being cut off by the tide. I don't think any of the wired pilgrims were paying their respects to Edgar Evans, the Polar packhorse, who died with Scott on the Ross Ice Shelf, as the fated party struggled back to base camp. A big man, born in Middleton, Rhossili, Evans was the first to go. Victim of a minor flesh wound that wouldn't heal. There is a memorial to the Petty Officer (First Class) in the Norman church of St Mary at Rhossili. Described as something of a naval traditionalist, a drinker and womaniser, Evans came close to being left behind in New Zealand, when, staggering aboard the *Terra Nova*, he fell into the harbour. Scott 'overlooked' the incident. He valued the Gowerman for his physical strength and for the stories he told.

The sweep of beach at Rhossili Bay, seen from the coast path or anywhere on the shore, was magnificent. The stretch of firm sand between Burry Holms and the erect tongue of Worm's Head was close to the distance of the entire cliff walk from Port Eynon Point to the Lookout

Station and the footpath to the village. But the reverse angle, looking from out at sea to the line of dunes, with the steep hill above, the burial mounds and single white house, was not so inviting. This was a beach famous for its wrecks. Returning to Rhossili with the two other teenage lads, at the time of our caravan holiday, after we'd done the walk with the girls, we climbed into a rusted freighter that had gone ashore and was now wedged at a dangerous angle in the sand. The risk of it seemed to sit alongside the crawl into the cave at Culver Hole. Immortality of youth has its limits. Even then it struck me, as we made it safely back to ground, that I'd used up two strikes of a potential three, and it was time to husband risk.

Buses, we were told, ran to Port Eynon at regular intervals. This one was late and oversubscribed. It was the hour of returning school children and tired coast-path hikers. The driver was brusque. He scorned the Freedom Passes that had carried us from Liverpool to Hull, hopping on and off local services, always with courtesy and interest from uniformed officials and fellow passengers. Wales was another country, it seems. And, by the way, as if to spite us, and as we lurched away from the stop, the driver told us that we wouldn't be going to Port Eynon. We'd have to disembark at Scurlage and wait for the next service.

I wasn't having it. Setting Anna up on a bench with some refreshments, I took to the fields. The woman selling soft drinks and biscuits said that she thought there was a 'ramblers' path'. She had tried it once in her youth, but never again. My challenge was to bring the car back before the next bus arrived. Despite the usual destruction of footpath signs, blocked gaps in fences, herds of bullocks, I almost made it: jogging, sweating, muttering. Down through the white-walled town and the lifeboatman's statute in the churchyard, back to the now deserted car park.

The Port Eynon bus was pulling out as I screeched to a stop beside Anna's bench, where she was finishing the *Independent* crossword, oblivious to my antics. She liked the Friday setter, PHI. 'He's my favourite,' she said. 'The others are not so good. PHI has the best clues, funny and witty.'

The following day, we drove to Pennard, on our way to the Premier Inn in Swansea. I wanted to challenge my memories of the visit to Vernon Watkins. Hovering uncertainly at the Pennard crossroads, trying to fix a route from so many years ago, I spotted St Mary's Church, and decided on no particular evidence that this was where Watkins must be buried. And so it proved. The poet's ashes were returned from Seattle. The whitewashed building is a restored medieval structure with a square tower like a detail borrowed from a child's fort. Inside the church, on the north wall, is a memorial: VERNON WATKINS. POET. 1906–1967. 'DEATH CANNOT STEAL THE LIGHT / WHICH LOVE HAS KINDLED / NOR THE YEARS CHANGE IT.' Above the granite slab is a specially commissioned icon.

Meandering in and out of new estates, crawling through mazy crescents and identical commuter units, in a constant fret of traffic, we took our time to reach the coast, and the car park I recognised from my original trip. Right beside the attendant's hut is a large detached property called *Heatherslade*. The Watkins house, where the family settled on his father's retirement from the bank, was still a retreat of sorts: an old people's home, with lawn and picture window, and grey plaque with gilded lettering. VERNON WATKINS LIVED HERE 1924 – 45. HE AND DYLAN THOMAS WROTE MANY POEMS IN THIS HOUSE.

While I was charging along the cliff path, staring dubiously at bungalows and villas, none of which quite conformed to my memory of the Watkins visit, Anna fell into conversation with the car-park attendant. A more fruitful line of attack. This lady was a reader. She said that she was rarely asked anything about Watkins or Dylan Thomas, but she knew where *The Garth* was to be found. And where we should search for the memorial set at the poet's favoured musing place. The rest where so many poems took shape.

We struck out for the second time. There were other bungalows that fitted better than the new building laid out in what was now established as the right place. Everything was changed. In the pub at lunchtime, beyond the nest of women discussing medical malfunctions, all 'hot and moist' in intimate places, there were only Australians in a camper van trying to locate lost relatives. The bungalow where I sat talking to the sharp-eared poet in his bed was fixed in another film. But I was free to do what was impossible then, in the gloom of the night: I could explore the paths where the poet walked. A rim of shingle and sand was squeezed between lumpy rock pavement and the first red ridges.

I missed the plaque. Anna, moving quietly and carefully, pausing to look down at where I was bounding from stone to stone, or hacking through spiky gorse, caught her breath against the slab we were searching out. The granite memorial

with its touched-up black lettering quotes those Vernon
Watkins lines from 'Taliesin in Gower'. 'I have been taught
the script / of the stones, /and I know the tongue of the
/ wave.' When the poet, coming here again and again, until
there was no 'here', no separation from place, wrote about
'Hunt's Bay', he said: 'The centre is never attained.' The sea
was in dialogue with things lost, returned, and lost once
more. 'The winds are mad about this time.'

After the Paviland bones in their cabinet of curiosities in
Swansea Museum, the handful of sea shells and mollusc cases,
the faded Polar photographs, we retreated to a Premier Inn
set down among unresolved marina developments around the
sorry relics of a working harbour.

On the final morning, before climbing into the car for our
return to London, we walked over dock bridges towards an
invasion of high-rise flats built among the dunes. And we fell
into conversation with the only other human moving through
this liminal territory. A young man, with a Cyclops-eye wedged
in his forehead, punted rapidly towards us on a set of ski poles.
He was like an anorexic, speed-crazed avatar of Edgar Evans,
turning the customised wilderness of Swansea Marina into an

Antarctic theme park. I thought the single red eye was a torch, allowing the Lycra-sculpted jogger to carry on through the night. His knees were gone. He was elasticated at every joint. But Anna was right. The blinking eye in the forehead was a camera. We were being recorded. We were part of his story. Two wildly different coast-path expeditions had collided in a landscape where neither party wanted to linger.

The man welcomed our intervention. Perhaps he needed material for the diary he was recording. He had set out from somewhere further to the west to run the entire coast path, marathon after marathon, bones ground to the brittleness of exhibits in the Paviland vitrine. Which was the madder project? He had a goal. When it was done, it was done. Feet up, he could watch the footage on a winter's night. My life's journey was just beginning, even though I was close to its chronological finish. Nothing happened, nothing was real until I tapped out the first sentence. I would begin with the Horton swim. The deserted car park. The dunes. Anna hugging her knees, dozing off, and thinking her own thoughts.

'Swallow at least a pint of water as soon as you're up in the morning,' one of the matrons in the Southgate pub told us, when we stopped for a drink on our way to Pennard. 'The secret of a long and healthy life. That and a sex episode at least once a year.'

It was done. Or so I believed. But dreams of Paviland stayed with me, unresolved. How was that to be managed?

RED LADY OF PAVILAND

Among the particulates spewed out by the chimneys of Margam, the eternal flames and black smoke-serpents of the apocalyptic steelworks flanking the M4 on the approach to Port Talbot, were the ashes of my parents. My father first and then my mother were cremated at Margam, an effectively managed facility between the streaming motorway and Eglwys Nunydd Reservoir with its sailing club. Some people confused this manmade lozenge of water, bordered by road and railway, with the much older Kenfig Pool, a nature-reserve lake sustained by legends of a drowned settlement, another variant on *La Cathédrale engloutie* by Ceri Richards. But the ancient borough of Kenfig was as much buried by sand as sea. Storms and exceptional tides, between the thirteenth and fifteenth centuries, devastated the coastal settlement. The conjunction of sun and moon in 1433, an event that occurs once every 1,700 years, was taken as an omen. The period is described, on information boards around the present pond, as a 'mini Ice Age'. The overgrown stub of the castle tower, out among the dunes, is all that remains of a once thriving community.

More potent than climactic or archaeological accounts

of the disappearance of this settlement were the myths and
legends that accumulated around Kenfig Pool. That there
was a city beneath the lake. That church bells could be heard
on the wind. That the inundation was divine punishment
for the robbery and murder of a steward carrying gold
to the local potentate, a certain Lord Clare; a fortune that
became the assassin's marriage fee. When a child of the
ninth generation of the original killer was born, there was
a great storm in the night. A black lake was discovered in
the place where the proud city once stood. Three chimneys,
rising from the water, were all that remained of the public

buildings, farms and households. They belched out noxious
fumes as a perpetual warning, a broken alphabet in yellow
smoke. A favourite book of my childhood came back to
me, *The Red Dragon and Other Stories of South Wales*, retold by
Brenda Girvin. 'The smoke smelt so unpleasant that he had
to turn away because it made his nostrils smart. When he
looked again at the lake, the chimney-tops had gone.'

It was March 4, our forty-eighth wedding anniversary, and

it felt right to be travelling west again, as we had, in the early-spring sunshine, all those years ago, when we returned to Dublin. This was the moment, if there was ever going to be one, for paying my respects to the Paviland Cave. Whatever the story was, in terms of my relationship with place, where I came from and where I was going, this Gower cave – the funnel sounded by Vernon Watkins, the receptacle for the black apples of Ceri Richards – held the secret. It had been important, I now recognised, on all those other expeditions, to find some excuse to keep the Goat's Hole in reserve. To wait. To make that missing piece the excuse for the next trip. Another walk. More photographs. This time there would be no tramping from Port Eynon to Rhossili. I would head directly to Foxhole Slade and the steep gully that ran down to the beach.

I wanted to break away from the drive to Oxwich Bay, where we would be staying before our latest Gower hike, to investigate Kenfig Pool, to see if any connection with the drowned cathedrals of Ceri Richards could be established. Those paintings are about looking *down* into the distorting clarity of water. But experiencing Kenfig Pool, from the car park alongside the closed Nature Reserve building, involves looking *across*: a classic panorama of sand dunes, mainline railway, motorway, and rounded shoulder of hills with ruined church above Margam Abbey. The freshwater lake, until you come right to it, seems diminished, a village pond or colliery feeder. At the water's edge, pond stretches into inland sea, with submerged woods and solitary trees, lapped by wavelets, like vestigial traces of lost islands.

Anna leans forward to taste the water, almost falling in.

'Brackish.' Iron. Rust. Reeds. Thickets of bare branches spidery above the wind-combed lake. A big blue sky with puffs of mammary anvil cloud. Where Anna stands, there is no drop into clear, cold water. Kenfig Pool is a flooded meadow. You think you can see wavering grass and spoiled crops submerged beneath the force of some winter storm, a river that has broken its banks.

Many of the paths around the lake have become streams. We find a bird-watchers' hide, and meet a rather furtive couple, solidly fleshed and slow moving, coming away from it. The letterbox slit of the hide reveals not a single duck, gull or seasonal passerine. The three smoking chimneys of legend do not rise from the depths, they are part of the perpetual fug of a heavy-industry horizon out beyond the dunes. Generous screws of Kleenex tissue are scattered across the cold floor. The hide reeks of wood preservative and cold semen.

Rabbits, commercially farmed, spilled into the dunes. Banks of ferns and sandy paths leading to mounds that might once have been outlying castle walls summoned memories of my prep-school walks, a couple of miles down the coast in Nottage. The essence of a landscape of burrows, earthworks, concrete pillboxes, barbed wire, was unchanged. Sixty years ago, I'm sure that I anticipated this afternoon. I was looking for the right warren in which to hide. The gritty taste of the air still painted the tongue a dull red. There were no words to do justice to the unlanguaged persistence of the Bristol Channel. Its puckered mantle and sudden rages. October waves breaking over the pier at Porthcawl, trying to float the giant apple of Coney Beach.

My parents were married in Llan, but they were not buried in that crowded ground with my maternal grandparents. And most of their neighbours from Neath Road. My mother made it clear that she favoured cremation. A gesture, perhaps, at the fashion initiated by the latter-day druid, Dr William Price, who incinerated his infant son, Iesu Grist

(Jesus Christ), in January 1884, on a flaming pyre at the end of a field commonly used for football, on the hillside above the village of Llantrisant. The location was pointed out every time we made a family drive from Maesteg to Cardiff.

Price's father, another William, was a clergyman whose eccentricities stood out even among that spectrum of oddities sheltering in parsonages across the country. The Reverend Price, like Emanuel Swedenborg, plunged naked into local pools and mud holes, cooling the fever of his religious ecstasies. He kept snakes in his pockets and carried a saw to carve bark from trees, which he later burnt, muttering ritual incantations. He spat on stones to validate them. And he carried a pistol.

The younger William trained as a surgeon, living for a time near St Paul's on the edge of the City of London, and attending the London Hospital in Whitechapel. The epiphany came when Price, a Welsh Nationalist, Chartist and political dissident, was in temporary exile in Paris. Visiting the Louvre, he discovered a stone with a Greek inscription that he believed represented an ancient bard making obeisance to the moon. Very soon he was interpreting the inscription as the prophecy of an invented Celtic prince. It was his duty, the doctor decided, to return to his native land and to free it from the cultural domination of English colonists. To this end, he invented his own form of Welsh.

There were ceremonies at the Rocking Stone in Pontypridd.

Price stalked the abused hills carrying a moon staff engraved with letters and figures. He wore a strange one-piece green costume, of his own design, which made him look like a gold prospector in a Sam Peckinpah movie. On his head was a trapper's fox-fur hat. He cultivated a long white beard and refrained from cutting his hair. He led a parade through the streets of Merthyr Tydfil, accompanied by a half-naked man calling himself Myrddin, and a goat. But all these picaresque flourishes do not amount to a true portrait of a man outside his own time: the era of scientific rationalism, canals, quarries, railways, telegraph, newsprint, Darwin and Marx. Performing on the cusp of the first papers published by Sigmund Freud, Price tapped visionary currents. He was a damaged shaman outside the system of the tribe. If the weight of history, as legitimised by museums and salaried academics, did not support his cosmology of need, like William Blake he would invent his own. Price learnt to trust his hunches. The truth was whatever he needed it to be. Fire cleansed all faults. When his time came, on the night of January 23, 1893, he called for a glass of champagne. He was cremated on a two-ton stack of coal, on the hillside above Llantrisant, in a ceremony witnessed by 20,000 people.

Attendance at Margam, for the cremation of my mother, was more modest. Fewer than for my father, two years before. Their friends were older, unwell, reluctant to travel. People slip very rapidly, when they retire or move a few miles closer to the sea, from the memory of place.

After Kenfig Pool, and before our return to Gower, we drove under the motorway and along the high-hedged approach to the crematorium. The abrupt turn in towards the tidy memorial gardens carried us right past a set of active smokestacks and cooling towers. We debated, without resolution, the precise spot at which the ashes of my parents had been scattered. Flattened bunches of flowers, with early daffodils, lay on the grass around a tree that Anna favoured. I thought the more pertinent memorial was the view from the car window. The throb of road miles in the metal. A nice prospect of name plaques around a semi-circular path to be studied, over a flask of tea, and a paper plate of cakes and sandwiches: that was their way. Binoculars, newspaper. Leaving the walking to impetuous youth.

The white concrete buildings, angular chapel and chimneystack, had the slightly sinister modernist aspect of those facilities that combine garden-city utopianism, country-park sculpture gallery and state-sanctioned prison. The officials are obliging and schooled in tact. We are led to the chapel where, colour-splashed from stained glass windows, folio Books of Remembrance are kept in glass cases. Gold capitals and blue italic calligraphy.

> Then I that here saw darkly in a glass
> But mists and shadows pass,
> And, by their own weak *shine*, did search the springs
> And course of things. . .

Lines I chose from Henry Vaughan: 'Resurrection and Immortality'. Outside, small boats with red sails tacked across the ruffled waters of the reservoir to which my father brought our dinghy, after the caravan in Horton was sold. Black smoke drifted inland over scorched hills.

The room they gave us in the Oxwich Bay cottage was called *Penrice*. It stood between *Horton* and *Paviland* – or the twin pillars of our repeated expeditions. The known and the unknown. Beach and cave. A good place, then, to slump into the sleep of incubation, after the road miles, pond and crematorium, and before the final attempt to access the site of the Early Upper Palaeolithic burial. The Red Lady-Boy. The cottage was also a kennel, pets welcome. Unseen, they sniffed and scratched and growled. Tomorrow there would be wedding guests.

A fat-cheeked moon, like a drinker's sweaty chalk face that has taken one punch too many, floated over the wide sweep of the bay. The never-darkened Swansea littoral, and the industrial strip beyond, twinkled in the distance, without disturbing the depth and serenity of country sleep. The crenellated fourteenth-century tower of the church of St Illtyd was built, so it is said, on the site of the cell of a sixth-century hermit. It dominated the dim headland: gravestones of the named, and slabs for those without names, pulled from the sea, glowed under a wash of orange lichen brighter than the markings on a London Overground carriage. The evening was soft and smelled of woodsmoke.

In a self-conscious room propped up with the peeled trunks of sturdy trees, and featuring rough-stone walls and an open fire, in loose tribute to an off-highway diner somewhere between Seattle and Eureka, we plotted tomorrow's walk. To allow ourselves time to search the cliffs for the Goat's Hole Cave, we wouldn't set out from Port Eynon, but park in the village of Pilton Green and then strike off across the fields to Thurba Head, exploring every promising slade and gully.

It was a quiet night in the restaurant. One couple, in the silence of wearied intimates, sat across from each other on chairs swathed in white bandages, flicking at competitive iPhones, and trying to call up images of the walk they had

Your Aura reading from Psychic Sarah

☻ My Aura – BLUE ☻

Most often seen in healers and very caring people.
Can indicate selflessness, talent in herbalism, or
spiritual or creative people, Light blues appear in the
auras of religious or spiritual people and also in those
with musical talent.
Deep blues show up in the auras of psychic people or
those with natural gifts to understand others.
Creative people will sometimes be seen with shafts of
blue light coming out of them.

Your Lucky Numbers: 19,40,42,23,11,25

DATE: 31/07/04

For amusement only

just completed. A tailored persuader with eye-catching talons was trying to sell a wedding package to a family business party. Tomorrow's bride, hair piled like an Egyptian headdress in brutal curlers, accepted a burger with a bucket of chips. The *maître d'* didn't trade on that unctuously insincere Mediterranean choke of welcome, or Parisian *froideur*. In an unaccustomed suit, and with a pleasing aura of having been dragged from his tractor and pressed into service, he grabbed plates in large hands and monkey-wrenched disobedient cutlery. The owners were working very hard to exploit the accident of the perfect seaside setting.

Every gate was a Passchendaele puddle churned by the delicate hoof prints of sheep. We slurped seaward through a low fret. It wasn't raining with intent, but chilled condensation ran from our arms and shoulders. Field margins dipped into secret holloways roofed with thorn and dressed with wool like beards of solid ectoplasm. Thurba Head, to a degree I had not previously recognised, was loud with traces of remote settlement: mounds, pits, sites of occupation and burial. Pushing on, rolling over locked gates, scraping off mud, we achieved the Gower Coast Path. And encountered one walker, a young man heading east with a long black bag that might have contained a set of pool cues or a hunting rifle.

The first slade I attempted, hoping for a sight of the cave marked 'Red Chamber', was a tumble, a nervous crouch. A thin green line, snaking down through rufous bracken, dropped abruptly into the world and time of stone. Slices of grey dusted with yellow lichen. A savage, elemental theatre of absence. I thought of Blake and his late, unfinished engagement with Dante. And one plate in particular, from 'Hell Canto 24', where the two poets, Dante and Virgil, are making their stiff-backed way out of the Pit of Hypocrites: 'The Laborious Passage along the Rocks.'

Here was a ledge on which to witness white water foaming on torn outcrops. Caves in the cliffs. The headland is a helmet of stone under a slick varnish of grass. I can identify the dark shadows of splits and faults, weathered cavities, but I can't nominate any workable angle of approach. If I made it to sea level, I would face another climb towards an overhanging lip, and a painful, inch-by-inch transit across the cliff face. The laborious passage in the wrong kind of hell.

Anna is waiting on the path. Standing here, it's hard to believe that there is a cliff path, fields, sheep, a busy road. The musculature of the forces in play is extreme and indifferent to human nuisance. When the folk above gouged out their shallow declivities, heaped up their burial mounds, the sea was remote, seventy miles out. But the pounding rhythms infiltrated the caves, while streams chiselled at rock. Hyenas were first, before bears. And hungry men.

We come to Foxhole Slade with a sense of recovery, having paused by the signpost above the scree-dresssed valley on a number of previous walks. It was never quite right to make the detour, without the confirmation that this was indeed the point of access to Paviland Cave. It was like standing, at last, in the nave of a cathedral whose doors were never open. The narrowing perspective drew the eye to a hit of polished light from the hidden sea. The signpost predicted the routes for Port Eynon, Rhossili, and inland to Pilton Green, but nothing was shown for Paviland. Tourists, bone-scavengers and pagans were not encouraged.

We set off, following a dry stonewall. Strands of barbed wire had been stretched along the top to keep pedestrians in their permitted pens. Where the wire had been cut, there

were torn scraps of cloth, crumpled cigarette packets; visible proof that walkers had skipped over the wall in order to reach a small cave on the other side of the slade. I followed. And discovered traces of earlier inhabitants: a circle of stones set for a fire, a tarpaulin sheet and a Smirnoff vodka bottle. This might be the only cave I would enter.

Now the shape of the headland was distinct, an altar of grey Carboniferous limestone. We advanced as far as the path took us, and then, once again, I edged over spines and sharp fins of rock towards the beach. The Goat's Hole was not to be seen from the furthest point I achieved without risking broken bones. That old phrase came back to me: 'You'll never make old bones.' I'd made them, old enough but not yet museum quality, and I wanted to keep what I had, chipped and bruised, encased in flesh.

This was the place. I felt the cave but I couldn't look at it or photograph it. The promontory itself, with its golden lichen crown, had unshaken presence. Anima. Spirit. A suitable backdrop in which to enfold the black apples of Ceri Richards, the generative sac. The pouch of shells and owl feathers. I thought of the prophet-seer, Taliesin, summoned by Vernon Watkins. 'Ah secret place,' he wrote. 'And there are three about me where I stand.'

But there was only one today: Anna pointed out a narrow crevice between cliff and path, a chain of razor rocks and cloudy pools. A possible route, but trickier perhaps than the abseil across the headland suggested by a stile leading to a well-used path.

I struck out, went down on all fours, tobogganed in the dirt, felt the space below me, and crept along a ridge that led nowhere, a sheer drop. Beaten, I retreated, retraced my skidmarks. Now there were three figures in conversation by the stile. A woman and a young man, winding down the ravine towards the sea, had stopped to talk to Anna.

It was the optimum moment, the woman explained, the tide was out. She was going to Paviland Cave. And would be sliding, without dignity, but very efficiently, on her bottom. She had done it many times before. And we would be welcome to follow.

Anna decided to retreat to the signpost, to eat an apple, to wait for me there. I followed my guide. I pushed to keep up across the smooth wet stones and around the lips of the chain of pools. The young man with the white plastic bag skipped from spur to spur. The woman in blue, her hair in a pigtail, Native American fashion, stayed right behind him, without appearing to make any special effort. I laboured, panting, not giving the rock pools the attention they deserved for fear that this magical couple, priestess and acolyte, would disappear into cliff or sea.

'Moon milk,' the woman laughed. 'Mermaids swim through this gully at high tide. And express their milk to feed the watersnakes.'

The pools were clouded mirrors in a descending chain. Their colours were subtle and preternatural, ranges of blues and greys giving life to the skin of the stone.

Without warning, I was translated into an entropic vision, a dream I recorded shortly before making the Gower walk with Brian Catling in 1973. Then, as now, it was March. The text of the dream became part of *Red Eye*, a book written at that time, set aside, lost, not published until 2013. I recognised the system of pools I was now crawling down, in the Paviland gully, as evidence of the route not taken on the Catling expedition. The map we were not yet ready to use.

One of my companions dives into a pool. I follow, my shoulder

towards home, memory. A chain of ponds, connected . . . The
water is dark and thick with plant tangle. I cannot climb out
so easily . . . Grey and green deaths are swimming towards me.
The rock that surrounds the pond is made from snakes. Their
bodies slide into cracks and fissures. They move their heads. Acid
menace, time streaks.

There is no valid interpretation of the evidence of
the cave, of the whole terrain, not for me: *what happens is
recognition as a form of possession.* Whatever has to be said,
with painstaking effort, research, is inadequate, when
positioned against the *life* of the stones; the traces of
origin scratched from rubble, midden pits, reserves of
long silence.

From the shoreline, the cave was partly obscured
by a thick outcrop, up which my guides were already
scrambling. You would have to go back some distance

to get the photographs that appear in guidebooks.
They speak of Goat's Hole as being 'pear-shaped', an
invocation of hidden 'Venus' figures with fatty deposits

on their hips and obvious fecundity. A shrine to the Mother Godess. It does not strike me that way. The dark, teardrop aperture is as sharp as a flint: a cutting tool, a flesher. From the hot plain inhabited by bison, rhinoceros, hyena and lion, this headland with its trapezoid crown, its yellow lichen crust, stood out as a golden cap. The cave was the eye of the Cyclops. A place for chewed bones and mysteries.

The sea could catch unwary visitors, my guide explained. One TV crew had to wade for it, while the director, unwilling to salt-stain his precious boots, tried to claw his way up the cliff. Exceptional tides lapped against the cave. Pools in the rock were rusty yellow and flickering with tiny see-through fish. The walker with the long black bag was leaving as we approached. When he was safely grounded on the limestone pavement, he stood staring out to sea for a long time; uncertain, after the experience of the cave, about where he should go next. Or perhaps he was waiting until he had the cave to himself.

The interior was tall and vaulting, sure of its continuing potency despite the nuisance raids of a procession of very determined pilgrims. My guide pointed out the spot, a nest of grey stones up against the damp green wall, where it was supposed that the Reverend William Buckland excavated the ochre-stained bones of the 'Red Lady' in January 1823. It was quite a story. And frequently told, I imagine, by the woman who brought me here. She lived, so she said, in 'mid Gower'. The drama of 1823 – a year when William Blake was living in his final chamber at Fountain Court, just off the Strand, and John Clare was venturing to London – was as vivid to

her as current news from Gwent of treasure hunters bidding
blind for the contents of repossessed storage containers,
or the death of 'New Romantic' Steve Strange, who would
be interred with all due ceremony, coffin supported by Boy
George and Martin Kemp, in Porthcawl.

Buckland was summoned from Yorkshire, where he had
been sorting hyena bones in Kirkdale Cave. He was forced
to yield, up there, to the evidence of the ossuary floor: that
animal devoured animal, and each brittle layer represented a
generation of predators and victims, and not proof of the
Biblical flood, with random remains carried from the tropics
on a tidal surge. Gower caves were known and investigated by
gentlemen with time on their hands, a surgeon and a parson
from Port Eynon. The curiosity of interested amateurs
carried through the groundwork that made it possible for
Buckland to sweep in and claim the glory. Mammoth bones
and other finds at Goat's Hole convinced the native pair that

it was imperative to alert the great Oxford palaeontologist. Who made his urgent winter journey. And took up residence on the Penrice estate, the property of the significant local landlord.

The eccentric Anglican theologian, wrestling with fundamentalist religious doctrine, and contradictory theories based on the work of spade and geological hammer, was a scholarly coprophile. Buckland pretty much invented the word. He championed the study of fossilised faeces as a method of dating ancient ecosystems. And he coined the term 'coprolite'. When he married, two years after the discoveries in the Paviland Cave, he improved his new home with a table inlaid with dinosaur coprolites. He was also a zealous devourer of the animal kingdom. A safari-park glutton. He munched through the specimen catalogue from panther to rat, puckering his lips a little over mole and bluebottle fly. The creationist was a man of iron will, racing towards clinical insanity. He snacked his way up Darwin's fraudulent evolutionary ladder. When he had done with fish and fowl, horse, cattle, monkey, mouse, bee, worm, louse and lizard, he happened, at Nuneham House, a Palladian villa outside Oxford, on the heart of a French king, purported to be Louis XIV, preserved in a silver casket. Before his hosts could move, Buckland swept up the dish and gagged down the rancid relic like a dubious oyster.

For palaeontological fieldwork, the notorious bone-botherer favoured full academic robes. Not quite forty-years-of-age, well into his maturity, as it was thought at the time, Buckland was a man of tremendous physical energy. And despatch. He came to Goat's Hole across the icy cliffs, as the

Penrice house party was recovering from Christmas.

The cave, beyond the area where the bones had been discovered, went back to a deep inner chamber, where the walls shone like meat left to rot; a brilliant phosphorescent viridian run through with veins of butchered red.

'Not ochre,' my guide told me, 'iron ore.' Red ochre was prized, but its usage was not necessarily ritual. The substance, a natural earth, was a preservative; it cleaned wounds. It was also a cosmetic used in body painting. It repelled insects. And helped to disguise the stench of decomposing bodies. The red of the bones of the young man of the Early Upper Palaeolithic in Paviland Cave might not have been dyed with ochre before burial, the colour could have leeched through from his garments or death wrap.

Ronald Hutton of Bristol University, an authority on ancient, medieval and modern paganism, discussed the matter, along with other pertinent observations on Paviland Cave, in his 2013 book, *Pagan Britain*. 'A few further observations can be made. The first is the great importance that people of the period attached, in ritual contexts, to the colour red. It is, of course, that of the vital fluid of life, which is also, in menstruation, the sign of human fertility. The costume of the Red Lady has already been noted, and other burials from the European Old Stone Age were given the same hue, either by sprinkling or painting with red ochre or likewise being interred in red clothing.'

There were no obvious paintings in Goat's Hole. Deer figures were found elsewhere in Gower. Professor Hutton points out that contemporary notions of sexual identity are not applicable to the revelations in the caves: gender is optional. Dancers or hunters enjoy male and female characteristics. So Buckland, in his determination to extract a scarlet woman, Roman prostitute or Stone Age witch, was not in error: he was premature, anticipating a more sophisticated view of the projection made from the evidence of the bones. Gender is plural, it leaks and flows. It is not possible, at this distance, to impose a rationale, by way of radiocarbon dating or comparisons with the behaviour of recorded Aboriginal groups, on the rituals of Palaeolithic people who left their bones in limestone caves. The otherness, despite DNA chains linking Cheddar Gorge excavations with contemporary schoolteachers, is absolute.

In Goat's Hole – and where are the goats? – we touch the dream of it. We are permitted to prod at the primitive within ourselves. The totality of place is dizzying. The shamanic drawings in other chambers, such as the famous 'Sorcerer' of Trois Frères in the Pyrenees, were not always intended to be seen. *They were made.* The making was the act. The purpose of this cinema of stones remains a secret, open to speculation, or revision by such as Abbé Breuil, whose copy of the 'Sorcerer' makes an entirely new artwork, a clarification of the multiple superimpositions of creatures and sexual identities gathered in one outline. The cave walls, with their natural fissures and emphasised cracks, their glistening meaty surfaces, Hutton tells us, were seen as 'membranes between human and other worlds'. Spirit forms, existing on the far side of the rock barrier, are solicited, brought into the conversation. The person making the drawing, at that moment, becomes the energy he is guided to depict. Patterns of migration and survival routines can be surmised, the spirits have departed.

Hunting rituals, ceremonies of primitive surgery, flesh stripped from bone in cannibal feasts, are fanciful scenarios proposed by academics on the evidence of raids on remote places. For myself, the swiftest passage to the culture of the caves comes through the visionary prose of a contemporary author who never reached the point where I am now standing: Brian Catling. At the start of his epic novel *The Vorrh*, a hunter makes a weapon. 'The bow I carry with me, I made of Este.' Forest-born, the dead female seer is processed into a new state of being and usage: 'divided and stripped into materials and language'. The hunter explains: 'I shaved long, flat strips from the bones of her legs. Plaiting sinew and tendon, I stretched muscle into interwoven pages and bound them with flax. I made the bow of these, setting the fibres and grains of her tissue in opposition . . . I removed her unused womb and placed her dismembered hands inside it. I shaved her head and removed her tongue and eyes and folded them inside her heart . . . My tasks finished, I placed the nameless objects on the wooden draining board of the sink. They sat in mute splendour, glowing in their strangeness.'

The cave glowed too, but its strangeness was not strange to me now. I thought again of that Wurlitzer quote. 'Things are not as they appear. Nor are they otherwise.' The walls seemed to contain their own sources of reserved light. And the shape of the day, through the black aperture, was utterly remote. My guide, the woman in blue, showed me a sharp-edged flint she had found on the cliffs above. It was hard to come across such things. New Labour had hurled money at this heritage coastal stretch in the heady millennial days, requiring frantic excavators to emerge with a bright new narrative, a prehistory of ecologically sound, premature Blairites. When there is nowhere left to invade, colonise the past. Held up to daylight, the flint was the precise shape of the cave's entrance; razor-rimmed and coming to a point.

There were high ledges, incubation compartments in which to tap the communal dream, to hold congress with spirits of place. My guide confirmed the acoustic properties. She said that a storyteller, standing with his back to the cave's entrance, could be clearly heard in the deepest recesses, but he would remain inaudible to those outside. It was also confirmed that the dating for the red bones had been pushed back, to 36,000 years.

My guide was well informed, comfortable in moving around the spaces of the cave. She knew all about Buckland's original discovery. His greed for objects: bones, shells, broken wands. His greed for explanations to justify the established faith in which he was a salaried minister. The daughters of the big house were swung down from the cliff face in large baskets. Which they filled with curious plunder.

The young man who accompanied the woman in blue stood waiting. His white plastic bag was open, revealing a selection of sugary drinks, crisps, chocolate bars. It was time for me to leave them to whatever it was they had come here to do. I told them a little about the book I was trying to write. My guide replied that her partner was also a writer. His name? 'Ronald Hutton.' Paviland Cave was a big subject for the scholar from the other side of the Bristol Channel. I searched out a copy of *Pagan Britain* as soon as I returned to London.

I had read, before this latest trip, that the jumble of bones and bits in Swansea Museum I had taken for bounty from Goat's Hole, reburied in a dusty cabinet of curosities, was nothing of the sort: replicas, frauds. The authentic Buckland findings were lodged in the University Museum in Oxford.

So my quest was not quite over. There was one last trip to be made. Photographs suggested a scientific display, discrete compartments for each of the elements. There was something to be said for the dusty theatre of Swansea Museum, the relics of fairground freak show, but I knew I wouldn't be satisfied until I followed Buckland back to base, among the rites and privileges of the golden city on the Jurassic causeway.

Looking into the background of Roland Hutton, it seemed

that my guide's name was Ana Adnan, yet another sonar echo in this story. My wife's maiden name was Anna Hadman. Anna reckoned that was about right. She brought me to the edge of the gully and pointed it out, before retiring to high ground and a bag of apples. The other lady manifested to lead me to the shape I had been searching for since that first initiatory teenage walk.

In *Pagan Britain*, Hutton proves a painstaking chronicler of the surviving manifestations of the Palaeolithic and Mesolithic periods – and the possible belief systems that lay behind the construction of mounds and monuments. He is clear that animating spirit must never be left out of the equation. The flow of time is nicely registered: that prejudices and politics of our own era direct the way that we interpret what we see as the past. The fetish for heritage. Inheritance. Ways of pollarding the messy family tree. My eye was caught by a description of post holes indicating that totem poles or honoured trees were allowed to rot before a long barrow was constructed on the same site. 'Potent symbols,' Hutton says, 'of birth, death and degeneration.' He goes on to point out how 'this metaphor reappears . . . at Haddenham in the Cambridgeshire Fenland, where a long barrow covered a long low timber structure . . . in which at least five people had been interred.' Christopher Evans and Ian Holder, authors of *A Woodland Archaeology: Neolithic Sites at Haddenham*, suggest that the process would have been like burial within a tree trunk.

Anna was struck by this report when I read it out. Her father's family, the Hadmans, had worked a small patch of land, on the dry rim of the Fens, for generations. Researching

Edge of the Orison, a book inspired by John Clare's 'Journey Out of Essex', we traced Anna's descendents as far as a marriage at the time of the French Revolution. They held their ground, peasant labourers to tenant farmers, schoolteachers, innkeepers and butchers. We helped to restore broken gravestones with lists of barely known connections. Did Hadman, the name, derive from Haddenham (Haeda's Ham) the place? DNA tests might link Anna to the flatlands in the way that contemporary Somerset folk were traced right back to the caves of the Cheddar Gorge. Five persons was our favoured family unit. The lift Anna always got from walking out onto Car Dyke, beyond Glinton, under those unforgiving skies, the wide horizons, the waterways, was the same confirmation I felt in Gower: being in the right place. But, in my case, with no sense of belonging. *Place itself bore more freight of meaning than any of the individuals on the tree of ancestors.*

Before we returned to Oxwich Bay, I wanted to pick up on a hint I found in the tribute Ceri Richards paid to his friend Vernon Watkins in the collection Leslie Norris edited for Faber, *Vernon Watkins 1906 – 1967*. As well as supplying a drawing of 'The Gower Coast from Pennard', Richards mentioned 'the heron often seen beside the river in the Castle Valley'. And how, one day, it alighted on Vernon's rough lawn. I thought if we could locate a vantage point above Three Cliffs Bay, which I visited with Anna before we were married, I could see if the river looked anything like the one that turns up in the lithograph derived from 'Poem in October' by Dylan Thomas. The one that hung in our kitchen.

This was National Trust land and there was nowhere to park. I left Anna in the car, wedged across somebody's driveway, and I walked down the lane until the beach came into view. Here was the Richards river without question.

There were no herons on duty. And the falling headless figure, tumbling under the black thumbprint of mortality, had to be imagined, like a shadow spilling across sand. The three points of rock that gave the beach its name were the profile of a giant sleeper: the head missing from the lithograph. The wriggling blue river was not the wide estuary at Laugharne as seen from the deck of the Boat House, it was much closer to the Richards holiday home, a good afternoon's walk out from Pennard.

The wedding in the Oxwich hotel was going well, the first ambulance had been summoned to the marquee. Dogs were fretting in our kennel, where one guest, shunting between *Horton* and *Paviland*, delivered an impassioned Ancient Mariner monologue from 3 a.m. to first light.

OXFORD

Swerving around a sandstone stump blistered with creatures, a neutered omphalos commemorating the site where Thomas Henry Huxley and Bishop Samuel Wilberforce debated Charles Darwin's *Origin of Species* in June 1860, I strode down the lefthand margin of the Oxford University Museum. While Professor Catling, a figure of substance in a swirling coat, paced the forecourt fielding the latest blizzard

of incoming iPhone nuisance. Between students, friends, publishers, agents, he was in constant demand. My guide to city and cloister, a respected dignitary from the Ruskin School of Drawing and Fine Art, was newly returned from London, where Allan Corduner, Arthur Sullivan in Mike Leigh's film *Topsy-Turvy*, had been recording a beautifully modulated version, with all the voices, of the madness of *The Vorrh*. Outside the glass booth, Catling watched, mesmerised, as his words came alive. The royal surgeon William Gull was vividly present as he thrust and parried through an interview with the cranially-challenged photographer Eadweard Muybridge. These elusive Victorians, like William Buckland and William Price, would not go away. They were our mentors and our tormentors. Behind the tangled beards and hats, they probed and promenaded.

Just beyond the high hall of the University Museum, a tremendous bone heap like the residue of Buckland's hungry assault on the animal kingdom, a set of stone steps drop into the darkened chamber holding the barely managed excesses of the Pitt Rivers collection. Alan Moore, in a high-necked jersey of ecclesiastical purple, and as fulsomely bearded as any Victorian magus, stood here to help launch *The Vorrh*, on its original independent press publication. He had climbed aboard his favoured mini-cab service in Northampton, wrapped himself in a familiar scarf of resinous smoke, and hit the road south. Holding the crowd of animated art fanciers in the palm of his hand, Alan drew the name of the lucky winner of a personally defaced copy of the book from a glistening top hat. But William Christopher Butler had just stepped out. Respects paid, Moore shook the paw of the proud author, kissed the relevant female persons, and headed home. Three hours absent from Northampton was an eternity never to be recovered. White Oxford drummers hammered away, invoking the voodoo of the forest, from

The Red Lady of Pavila

balconies of weapons and fetishes. Allan Corduner, I remembered, had played Verne in Nicolas Roeg's abortive television adaptation of *Heart of Darkness*, one of the more obvious inspirations for *The Vorrh*.

At the top of the Pitt Rivers steps, in the corner of the University Museum, a few yards from Alan Moore's head, was the cabinet containing the actual ochre-dyed bones of the Red Lady of Paviland. They pulsed in dim obeisance at the vibration of Alan's persuasive voice: the deep, thousand-year-old, smoke-saturated growl of Northamptonshire mud that required no DNA scrape to authenticate. The voice was older than the Gower specimen cupboard. It was, as Moore recognised in the title of his 1996 novel, a *Voice of the Fire*.

This first novel, perhaps a preliminary pass at the major excavation of locality that would become the endless Northampton epic, *Jerusalem*, shifted, era by era, through helixes of interconnected plural time. Infinity on the head of a cobbler's nail. The Neolithic hog pit, where ancestral voices are first registered, is contemporary with Roman invaders,

Cromwell, John Clare and Moore himself. The Paviland cabinet is silent. Moore's bones grunt and talk, thickly, in dialect, in ways the University relics refuse to condone. 'Low sayings come from white-skin hut.' Time loops and repeats. Fire is fiercely articulate. 'His blackened sockets stare as if to scry the smoke for messages . . . His skin flakes off to rise as great slow moths of ash into the firmament.'

I'd forgotten how Catling, described as a 'mesmerizing golem', enters Moore's script, coming to Northampton to read at the round church of Holy Sepulchre. A passage from *The Stumbling Block*, a mantic text of the London streets, provokes a member of the hushed audience, 'a sometimes homicidal medicine-head of local notoriety'. This oversensitive critic, after warming up with a little glass-chewing affray in the pub, spits bloody teeth on the pavement and rushes home to collect a gun. He stakes out the graveyard, in order to cull the poet before he can do more damage to a seething microclimate of barely managed anarchy and pint-swallowing socialist dispute.

Moore logged the episode as a minor speciality of place for those who could not afford motor vehicles or taxis: 'the stroll-by shooting'. Beneath all the knotted narratives of territory, as with Gower, lay hidden caves and cellars 'where fears and dreams accumulate'. The hilltop town of business was mined with the burrows of forgotten workers. Legions of the restless dead packed the tight passages like leathered mummies in the Capuchin Catacombs of Palermo. 'The underworld is literal, though occult,' Alan wrote, 'webs of tunnels lace the earth below the settlement.'

The display cabinet to which the partial skeleton from

Goat's Hole had been brought functioned like the concluding panel in a necklace of skulls, trophies ranging from amiable no-browed knuckle-draggers to humanoids primed to kill. I felt, quite strongly, that the Gower wanderer, after whatever hard miles he had stalked, as a hunter, on what is now the Atlantic seaboard, from the Pyrenees to Brittany and Cornwall, should be laid to rest. Returned to the horizontal plane and wrapped, once more, in ceremonial red cloth.

Parading the disarticulated bone sections of less than half a skeleton, half a young man, and referring to him as a scarlet woman, prostitute to a Roman camp, was a travesty. Less to do with scholarship than with the status of Buckland and the university. It is Buckland's portrait in the cabinet, frockcoat, top hat, umbrella and black bag, posed beside the wrong cave. The backboards of the display are a vibrant green, a denial of the winter greys and yellow lichens of Gower. The ilium of the recovered man has a hole, in the shape of Paviland Cave, punched through it, creating the profile of an alien creature, a man-animal hybrid, stalked by the vertical stem of his own femur. It is impossible to escape the suggestion that bones come from other species, the hunted, the extinct. The Red Lady is a necessary assemblage. The parts that are missing, stolen, carried away by predators, ground to dust and swallowed in occult ceremonies, sing in whatever sphere of existence they still inhabit. Buckland's theft undid the power of the original chamber.

Museum-approved images, making explanatory illustrations for children, catch the angle of the flint-shaped entrance to Goat's Hole very well, but the bearded, fur-clad burial group with their burning brands look more like Scott's fated polar party. Five shaggy men, with Rhossili's Edgar Evans guarding the entrance. The ritual involves spears and measuring wands to be laid in a lattice across the dead man's chest. The geography of the journey insists on *precisely* this position. And it is not to be undone by careless thieves of future generations. Catling, in the late seizure of *The Vorrh*, defines the aura of Paviland with characteristic precision. He recalls our 1973 walk, which came before the fateful hour when his memory was transferred to electronic devices. 'The cave's bare interior seemed at once empty and brimming with occupation. I curl into the sanctity of this most human shelf and taste the joy of its simplicity with the edge of my sudden tiredness.'

It's a neater, cleaner pitch now but the University Museum is an obvious extension of the cabinet of curiosities, the dusty vitrines of Swansea or the overstocked oddities gathered by the family of Lambeth plantsmen, the Tradescants, and carted to Oxford by Elias Ashmole. Racked beside the Paviland bones are shards of Victorian whisky bottles, ochre-stained artefacts, shells, ivory bracelets, pendants made from deer teeth. The whisky was needed, by early scavengers, to keep out the January chill, the bite of wind, waves crashing on limestone rocks. The initial discoveries in Paviland – or the first discoveries to be made public – were achieved in 1822 by names now forgotten by the public, those local enthusiasts, L.W. Dillwyn and Miss Talbot. William Buckland was summoned, to tell the story, to measure it against Christian fundamentalism. And to accept his own descent into madness. The University Museum is a fitting obituary in three dimensions. If you don't get it by simply wandering through the forest of bones, the dinosaurs and other great beasts stripped of their coats, the pitch is available on printed cards. So here is Buckland once again, finger stuffed in the heart of a coprolite, lecturing an excited audience on the wonders of Paviland Cave. Alongside this comic strip are the objects and instruments that confirm his status: the geological hammer, fossilised turds and fading publications of record.

Professor Catling, scholar and performer, loomed up behind me, digital devices gripped like six-shooters. They bleeped and flashed and whined. In black coat, with helmet of silver hair, spectacles and gravitas, he seemed like the last representative of that Victorian tradition. The current students at Ruskin, so he told me, do not spend time in the museums, absorbing as he did, the weight and density of the mute exhibits. Catling, like Ceri Richards and Vernon

Watkins before him, but at a very different temperature, got it all. The long apprenticeship. The hardwon craft. And the steady refusal to chase the bitch, fame. Except on his own terms. Catling's mortal hunts, as *The Vorrh* demonstrates, grind out their bitter paths across infinite tracts of time.

'His formidable skeleton had been broken and repaired

many times,' *The Vorrh* reports. 'He looked like a shadow in the room and perhaps he was.'

I drove down to Oxford early on the day of George Osborne's strategic pre-election budget, which he presented with all the slippery relish of a corrupt school prefect dodging the bullet by blaming voiceless victims. The latest outrage for Wales was aimed at Swansea. A billion-pound 'tidal lagoon' – check out the CGI version, like a showpiece Frank Gehry Guggenheim Museum with zero content – 'generating power to run 120,000 homes for 120 years'. They could, for minimal investment, have tapped the dynamo in the rocks, the generator of legends. And all of it run from a single person channelling the spirit of the cave. More madness for the Swansea Marina. More Premier Inns and tower blocks abraded by black sand from the shifting dunes. Ballardian lagoons are filled with income streams from money that does not yet exist, complacent government pumping in £90 – £95 of our tax harvest per megawatt hour of energy.

It needed a strong coffee in Brian's quiet house by the river, under the gaze of a goat's skull too large for its jar, to exorcise an image from the service station where I paused to plot my route through Oxford. A man sitting directly opposite me, in slurred conversation with a slumped couple of nighthawks forced reluctantly to the scummy surface of consciousness, exposed the rude curvature of his naked red buttocks, cysts, weeping buboes and black-crusted split, to full view. The sheer quantity of meat on display was an affront to vegans and carnivores alike. A waitress, with great delicacy, tried to pull down his coat, with only partial success, every time she passed the table.

There had been plenty of these expeditions in the old days. We were both too busy now with the lesser entanglements of occupied lives. There is much to be said for unemployment, a few weeks of casual labour in ullage cellar or graveyard and then the freedom to undertake any script, however deluded. Catling's house pulsed with projects, breakfast plates pushed aside to make room for his paintings. Books were shelved and immediately to hand. He picked out one of his cornerstone texts, not much inspected in recent times: Buckland's *Curiosities of Natural History*. This was not, as Brian suspected, the right

Buckland. It was Francis, the son, surgeon and popular natural historian. Young Frank, vigorously flogged through his private education, respected his father's inclinations as a pioneer of zoöphagy. He continued the tradition of gorging his way through the animal kingdom. Mice in batter, squirrel pie, horse's tongue. Buckland's London home, at 37 Albany Street, was part menagerie, part night kitchen. Tureens bubbled with folded sections of elephant's trunk, rattled with porpoise heads. He stewed mole. And squashed rhinoceros meat into a Desperate Dan pie.

We took to the Oxford streets, in the blessing of this golden morning, to hit the museums. My guide was a marked presence: he was saluted by a succession of confident young women and shuffling youths. On a bench, he noticed a ranter, a black man locked in a fevered soliloquy that had him twisting, shoulder-shrugging, and throwing out his arms in heretical semaphore. His demons were dangerously close to the surface of yellow malarial eyes. There was no community left to care. For the past few years, medicated and dumb, the man processed the labyrinth, between markets and sites of Marian barbecues. Now he might as well have been fixed in the stocks.

'The breakthrough for *The Vorrh*,' Brian said, 'wasn't a book. Not *Impressions of Africa* or *Heart of Darkness*. Not even *Blood Meridian*. It was technology. Getting a laptop. Discovering that I could write in bed. Open the lid and away it went. I took the dictation as fast as it came.'

In the Ashmolean, a genial man at the enquiry desk asked if I was Welsh. I thought all traces of origin had been smoothed away in the ridicule of an English preparatory school. But the man from Neath was undeceived. I told him that I came from Maesteg. 'We always beat you,' he said. Not so, I replied. My last game for Maesteg's Youth Team, when we topped the unofficial league under the captaincy of local legend, Chico Hopkins, was an honourable draw against those purse-grabbing blackshirts from the tin town.

Brian found what we were looking for: the copper alloy figure of a boar, date unknown, excavated from Goat's Hole. A rubbed-smooth toy, or badge from the book of founding legends, the tale of Culhwch and Olwen from *The Mabinogion*. 'In the highest wind in the world, they looked about them and they could see a great smoke towards the south, far off from them . . . Dillus the Bearded was singeing a wild boar.' When King Arthur asks the warriors if there are any 'marvels still unobtained', one of the men replies: 'There is: the blood of the Black Witch, daughter of the White Witch, from the head of the Valley of Grief in the uplands of Hell.'

Going outside, to field more calls, while I check the rack of postcards, Brian encounters another special face. A fine-featured man with clear Scottish eyes, wearing a green suit and clutching a wheely case, poised for flight.

Introductions. Desultory conversation. 'Jon'. A former Keeper of the Print Room, art historian at the Ashmolean, author of books on Ingres and Claude Lorrain. The surname escapes Brian. He has to stab at one his portable memory tablets. The more you draw on these reserves, the more your own cataloguing system leaks. 'Whiteley'. An Academy Juvenile Award child actor grown to a mildly surprised maturity. The younger self, suspended in the eternal present of film, never changes. While the older man, within the mask of time, retains the buried spark of fame. Dirk Bogarde, who mentored the Monymusk ingenue through Charles Crichton's *Hunted* in 1952, and co-starred with him once again in *The Spanish Gardener*, tried to adopt the boy. In retrospect, a lucky escape. Jon never wanted to return from California, despite being directed by the autocratic Fritz Lang in *Moonfleet*.

Perched on his bench beside the Ashmolean bus stop, Whiteley's highland gaze passed unobstructed through flesh and stone. I remembered Anna telling me, when we were on a cross-country bus trip of our own, that all the girls in Huyton, outside Liverpool, where she'd been sent to school, swooned over Dirk in *The Spanish Gardener*. The screening was a big mistake, sending illicit vapours sweeping through the sheltered single-sex community.

Before I dropped Brian off at Dorchester-on-Thames, he had a place he wanted to show me. He'd been taken with the black-and-white photographs I produced of our Gower walk in 1973. 'I look just like Jack.' His oldest son. Jack Ishmael, like Francis Buckland, was loping along in his father's considerable footsteps. Sometimes they worked together as performance artists. But Jack was now out there on his own.

We came away from the road in Nuneham Courtenay and down a private way that led to an imposing Palladian mansion: Nuneham House. The property, built for Simon, the first Earl Harcourt, is owned by Oxford University and leased as a Global Retreat Centre for Brahma Kumaris. This, Brian revealed, is where Buckland chewed up the French king's shrivelled heart.

There are discreet surveillance cameras on poles around

the car park and police incident tape on the abandoned tennis courts, but the property is otherwise submerged in mediated waves of world peace and corporate chanting. The kind that makes you very nervous. Like an episode of *The Prisoner* before the fun starts. The park, laid out by Lancelot 'Capability' Brown in the second half of the eighteenth century, still smarts under the imposed discipline of always appearing grand enough to impress visiting royalty. Something after the fashion of a private golf course attached to a Cotswold county-house hotel.

A hillock, overlooking the sacred Thames, believes that it is much more than a view. Oliver Goldsmith, who witnessed the demolition of the ancient village of Courtenay, torn down and removed, along with the surrounding farms, in order to create the quotably ornamental landscape, composed *The Deserted Village* as an angry response. In more recent times, a premature *Downton Abbey* flavour was achieved by the marriage of Lewis Vernon Harcourt, known as 'Loulou', to Mary Ethel Burns, a niece of the American financier and plutocrat, J.P. Morgan. Morgan offered his relative a line of credit at his London bank. It was used for renovation and improvements to the grounds.

A dark well, protected by a decorative ironwork lid, was purposefully avoided by Professor Catling. 'Badly tainted,' he said. 'Black water.' One of the male Harcourts, he couldn't remember which, was fished out, after a suspected suicide.

We approached the temple on the hill. All Saints had been established on the ruins of the Nuneham village church. Around the back, among tombstones, a primitive shelter had been erected to protect a family monument, a relic of the original church, from the worst of the weather. Badly eroded married sleepers. Their two children eaten away by time.

I had been warned of the negative impact of stepping inside, pulling open the grille-protected glass doors. Catling had visited, first, with an artist friend, on a pleasant summer's afternoon. They didn't need to speak. The atmosphere, as he explained, was paradoxical: 'dry wetness'. A lung-squeezing chill that brought unsuspecting tourists out in a cold sweat. The carpet seemed to have been laid across a squelching bog, not firm foundations. The monuments and funerary wreaths were blasphemous interventions. The church drained colour, drawing the reluctant eye down the aisle to a dim altar, in a migrainous grey-mauve wash, bleached by electrical storms.

It was when I tried to frame a photograph, back towards what was left of natural daylight, beyond the glass door, that I made the connection with Paviland. Catling nodded his approval. He had lined up a shot on his first visit and thought better of it. There are images you don't want to carry around. The church was close to the cave, but quite contrary in spirit. The proportions were much the same and the outside world was just as remote. But Goat's Hole had the integrity All Saints lacked. Its rituals were unreadable. If there were images scratched on the wall, they paled into cracks and natural faults. The chapel constructed for the glory of a single family, overseeing managed fields running down to the Thames, was a museum as much as a warriors' shrine. All Saints was the interface between Paviland Cave and the Pitt Rivers collection.

Once again, I remembered *The Vorrh*. There is a sequence, true to Catling's own habits and inclinations, where a tribesman, a hunter and suborned colonial exhibit, is brought to England, and taken to a great museum, where he is horrified to find photographic representations of his ancestors and captured artefacts that are their gods.

'It was the museum that changed everything and explained the volume of their lies. Like the churches he had been to, it was lofty and dark . . . They told lies – the scenes, the guide – about men, living in ice and sleeping with dogs . . . He had walked into a trove house of all that was significant, all that was cherished – all that was stolen.'

Before we drove to Dorchester, Brian insisted on a detour through the estate towards a set of farm cottages and sheds. He expected this place, as on his previous trip, to be deserted, quiet. But there are obvious signs of occupation, tractors readied for use. We turned back. He halted me again. The sun was low. He pointed to a patchwork of fields, pylons and solitary trees. And there was evidence of the hood of the uncanny that he carried around with him, along with those flashing, bleeping tablets that bore the burden of memory. All the names and faces and facts were stored in these wafers. Without them, he was thick-tongued, trapped in the ellipsis of his conquered stutter: neural impulses that flickered like a Maltese Cross in a cinema projector.

'The shadows,' I said.

'Yes, but . . . it's much weirder than that.'

The sun, depending over the river, threw shadows of the line of trees alongside the farm track over the fields in parallel lines. But out there, with no logic in physics, shadows of ancient oaks, left from the era of demolition, *ran the other way*. It felt as if the shadows preceded the structures to which they belonged.

When Brian parked here in the car of his friend, the painter Rebecca Hind, they noticed a psychic manifestation that belonged somewhere between their mutual but discrete zones of interest. There were three shadows in the burnt yellow of the field, well away from trees, pylons, hedges, *with no obvious source*. No aircraft overhead. No elongated clouds. The time of day, the heightened acuity of two artists trying to put the clammy grip of the private chapel behind them. Shadows, left by the phantom buildings of the ruined village, shapes of lost farms, should have been perceptible only on infra-red film, cameras sweeping the landscape from helicopter or glider. In the war years, Nuneham House was requisitioned by the Ministry of Defence and used by the RAF for interpretation of photographic evidence brought back from reconnaissance missions over enemy territory.

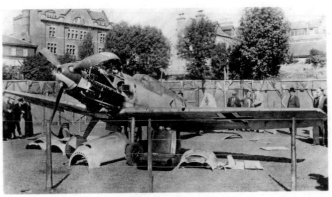

"MADE IN GERMANY — FINISHED IN ENGLAND."
MESSERSCHMITT M.E.109.
C.T. Photo.   ALL PROCEEDS GO TO OUR LOCAL SPITFIRE FUND.

Totes Meer. Paul Nash painted his frozen ice-sea of wrecked aircraft a mile or two down the road at Cowley. Like Rebecca Hind, he honoured the landscape and the special light of Dorchester-on-Thames. A partially eclipsed sun hangs above

that junkyard glacier of cut wings and crumpled fuselages in the apocalyptic dump. The vision could have been constructed from layer upon layer of reconnaissance prints from Nuneham House.

The eclipse of March 20, 2015, was on us. The shadows from that English field and the gravity of the Welsh cliff with its black apples were taking a heavy toll. Too many morning walks were to the hospital on the Hackney ridge above the buried river. Too many photographic interpretations were of fuzzy X-rays of rogue internal constellations. On a more farcical note, coming away from the silenced birdsong of the eclipse, that stillness when eggs can be balanced on a table, I was targeted by a non-signalling taxi near Liverpool Street. I dived out of its path at the cost of pulling and tearing every muscle I didn't know I had. Creeping the short distance to London Bridge took the rest of the day. It was suicide to try and cross a road, but you notice marvellous details in the fabric of the city that you would otherwise ignore. The world contracts to the muse of pain.

I checked that quote from Act 1, Scene ii of *King Lear*. 'These late eclipses in the sun and moon portend no good to us: though the wisdom of Nature can reason it thus and thus, yet Nature finds itself scourged by the sequent effects . . . We have seen the best of our time: machinations, hollowness, treachery, and all ruinous disorders, follow us to our graves!'

The three shadows from the Nuneham field were absorbed and worn like sergeant's chevrons. My understanding of the cave, clumsily expressed, was obtained at a price. Coming away from the Ashmolean, from the gleam of that brazen Paviland boar, and while the sanctioned priest of place, Professor Catling, paced in his black coat, animated by lightning jolts from slender digital tablets, summoning up child actors and city ranters, I scanned a carousel of postcards, to find something to bring home to Anna. I could barely make out the details of the one I chose, beyond a burdened ship of fools on a green sea, white sails pregnant with wind supplied by a cruising angel. *St Nicholas of Bari Banishing the Storm* by Bicci di Lorenzo (active 1380s – 1452). Tempera and gilding on panel.

This is what I needed: a device for banishing the storm.

The ship, packed as tight as a consignment of desperate asylum-seekers bound for Lampedusa, shudders in panic. Precious cargoes are hurled overboard. The bellying sail is in tatters. But the sea is running to nothing more than a force four swell. A naked woman with long gold hair, a sea witch floating just above the waves, swims away from the melon slice of the doomed ship's trailing tender. Nimbus-crowned Bishop Nicholas, against a studded ceiling of generic stars, offers his casual benediction, while cruising effortlessly on a kindly thermal.

One day with Brian had reminded me of the power of objects: bugs and bits in cabinets, fragments of Victorian whisky bottles, the bleached skulls of goats, well-thumbed pages of favourite books, photographs stalling time in false narratives, paintings-in-progress, remnants of a breakfast table, feathers, stones. And he reminded me too of the mysterious potency of place, under particular dispensations of light, with anecdotes of previous encounters refreshing the dim surface. Strings of bone, when they cross, create a shock of divine illumination. 'The skeleton,' as Richard Tuttle said on his card in the Whitechapel Gallery, 'because it was hidden, appears to have been exposed, almost inadvertently.' Almost inadvertently, we let the car drive us away.

Rooks mobbing bare trees, to override the din of builders, were waiting in Dorchester above the shed where Rebecca Hind kept her sketchbooks of black-sand beaches in Iceland: needled skies and dazzling Northern Lights. Trepanned visions without the smoking drill. Remembrances waiting on the right rememberer. And then, once more, with much to digest, I was back on the road. Of course nothing was resolved. One quest folded immaculately into the next as I drifted into the commuter traffic. The Paviland bones in the cabinet of the University Museum in Oxford were as phoney as the sandy splints in the glass coffin in Swansea. The validated remnants of the Red Lady were somewhere secure, boxed in the Museum basement. Or perhaps, as rumoured, returned to Wales. It didn't matter now. This letter was concluded. And there was still work to be done.

ACKNOWLEDGMENTS

First to Anna, for company and presence, early and late, in all of this. And for her ability to conjure fortuitous contacts and collisions out of empty landscapes and motorway corridors.

Then to Adrian Cooper at Little Toller for setting me on the road west, by inviting me to nominate a favoured place.

With thanks to Mel and Rhiannon Gooding for their hospitality and for making available rare items from the Ceri Richards archive. And for permission to quote from publications and to reprint significant images. The argument of the book would not hold up without this material.

Brian Catling came along, in 1973, on the walk that injected the territory into my eyeballs, and he was still around to smooth over my recent return to Buckland's Oxford and Nuneham House.

The monograph by Richard Burns on *Keys to Transformation*, published in 1981, sharpened my sense of the power of the 'Black Apple' as revealed through the paintings of Ceri Richards. This was a groundbreaking study.

For permissions, conversation, coffee, insights, challenges, I would like to thank: Renchi Bicknell, the late bookman/collector/publisher Alan Clodd, Mike Goldmark, Jamie Harris, Rebecca Hind, Jill Hollis, Jeff Johnson, Windsor Jones, Andrew Kötting, Clive Lewis, Alan Moore, J.H. Prynne, Will Shutes, Anthony Stokes and Jess Chandler of Test Centre, and my unknown guide to Paviland Cave. And, belatedly, Vernon Watkins. With special thanks to Gwen Watkins for permission to quote from the poems of Vernon Watkins and from her own memoirs.

SELECT BIBLIOGRAPHY

Allott, Kenneth, ed. (1950) *Contemporary Verse,* Penguin

Anderson, Jon (2014) *Page and Place: Ongoing Compositions of Plot*, Rodopi

Bicknell, Laurence 'Renchi' (1998) *Michael & Mary Dreaming (A walk along the Michael and Mary lines from Norfolk to St Michael's Mount in Cornwall),* Privately printed

Bicknell, Laurence 'Renchi' (2008) *A Pilgrim's Progress & Further Relations,* Privately printed

Blake, William (1969) *Complete Writings* (Ed. Geoffrey Keynes), OUP

Bowness, Alan and Robertson, Bryan (1981) *Ceri Richards* Catalogue for Tate Gallery

Burns, Richard (1981) *Ceri Richards and Dylan Thomas: Keys to Transformation,* The Enitharmon Press

Catling, Brian (1974) *Vorticegarden*, Albion Village Press

Catling, Brian (2015) *The Vorrh*, Coronet

Damon, S. Foster (1973) *A Blake Dictionary,* Thames and Hudson

Davies, Andrew (2012) *Walking on Gower,* Cicerone, Cumbria

Dunlop, Tessa (2015) *The Bletchley Girls*, Hodder

Gillham, Mary E. (1977) *The Natural History of Gower,* D. Brown, Cowbridge

Girvin, Brenda (1914) *The Red Dragon and Other Stories of South Wales,* Nelson

Gooding, Mel and Rhiannon, intro. (1984) *Ceri Richards: An Exhibition to Inaugurate the Ceri Richards Gallery,* University College of Swansea

Gooding, Mel (2002) *Ceri Richards,* Cameron & Hollis, Moffat

Gooding, Mel (2010) *Ceri Richards, The Poetic Imagination,* Jonathan Clark & Co

Grenfell, Harold and Morris, Bernard (2006) *The Caves of Gower,* The Gower Society

Guest, Lady Charlotte trans. (1877) *The Mabinogion (from the Welsh of the Llyfer Coch O Hergest),* Bernard Quaritch

Herd, David, ed. (2015) *Contemporary Olson,* Manchester University Press

Hill, Geoffrey (2010) *Oraclau / Oracles*, Clutag Press

Hutton, Ronald (2013) *Pagan Britain,* Yale University Press Jones, Gwyn and

Jones, Thomas, trans. with intro. (1949) *The Mabinogion,* Dent

Joyce, James (1939) *Finnegans Wake,* Faber

Mathias, Roland (1974) *Vernon Watkins,* University of Wales Press

McKrenna Rollie (1982) *Portrait of Dylan, A Photographer's Memoir,* Dent

Moorcock, Michael (2014) *The Whispering Swarm,* Tor Books, New York

Moore, Alan (1996) *Voice of the Fire,* Gollancz

Norris, Leslie, ed. (1970) *Vernon Watkins, 1906 – 1967,* Faber

Norvig, Gerda S. (1993) *Dark Figures in the Desired Country (Blake's Illustrations to* The Pilgrim's Progress), University of California Press

Ormond, John (1969) *Requiem and Celebration,* Christopher Davies

Richards, Ceri (1980) *Drawings to Poems by Dylan Thomas,* The Enitharmon Press

Richards, Frances (1982) *A Friendship, Vernon Watkins and Ceri Richards,* Privately printed for the Enitharmon Press

Sebald, W.G. (2012) *Across the Land and the Water (Selected Poems, 1964 – 2001),* Penguin Books

Sinclair, Iain (1972) *Muscat's Würm,* Albion Village Press

Sinclair, Iain (1973) *The Birth Rug,* Albion Village Press

Sinclair, Iain with Catling, Brian and Bicknell, Laurence (1973) *Albion Island Vortex,* Catalogue for Whitechapel Gallery show

Sinclair, Iain (2001) *Landor's Tower,* Granta Books

Sinclair, Iain (2013) *Red Eye,* Test Centre

Stephens, Meic, ed. (1986) *The Oxford Companion to the Literature of Wales,* OUP

Stewart, Barry and Grenfell, Harold (2000) *The Butterflies of Gower,* Gower Society

Thomas, Dylan (1939) *The Map of Love,* Dent

Thomas, Dylan (1940) *Portrait of the Artist as a Young Dog,* Dent

Thomas, Dylan (1952) *Collected Poems (1934 – 1952),* Dent

Thomas, Dylan (1954) *Quite Early One Morning (Broadcasts),* Dent

Thomas, Dylan (1955) *Adventures in the Skin Trade,* Putnam

Thomas, Dylan (1955) *A Prospect of the Sea (and other stories),* Dent

Thomas, Dylan (1957) *Letters to Vernon Watkins,* ed. with intro. by Vernon Watkins, Dent/Faber

Thomas, Dylan (1972) *Under Milk Wood (A Play for Voices),* with lithographs by Ceri Richards, The Folio Society

Thompson, David (1963) *Ceri Richards,* Methuen

Towns, Jeff, comp. (2006) *Vernon Watkins' Swansea,* Ty Llên Publications

Tucker, H.M. (1957) *My Gower,* Rowlands & Company, Neath

Watkins, Gwen (1983) *Portrait of a Friend,* Gomer Press

Watkins, Gwen (2005) *Dylan Thomas: Portrait of a Friend* (Revised edition with preface by author and foreword by Paul Ferris), Y Lolfa

Watkins, Vernon (1941) *Ballad of the Mari Lwyd,* Faber

Watkins, Vernon (1945) *The Lamp and the Veil,* Faber

Watkins, Vernon (1948) *The Lady with the Unicorn,* Faber

Watkins, Vernon (1954) *The Death Bell,* Faber

Watkins, Vernon (1955) *The North Sea* by Heinrich Heine (trans.), Faber

Watkins, Vernon (1959) *Cypress and Acacia,* Faber

Watkins, Vernon (1962) *Affinities,* Faber

Watkins, Vernon (1968) *Fidelities,* Faber

Watkins, Vernon (1977) *Elegy for the Latest Dead,* Privately printed for Alan Clodd

Watkins, Vernon (1979) *The Ballad of the Outer Dark,* The Enitharmon Press

Wurlitzer, Rudolph (2008) *The Drop Edge of Yonder,* Two Dollar Radio

Little Toller Books

We publish old and new writing attuned to nature and the landscape, working with a wide range of the very best writers and artists. We pride ourselves in publishing affordable books of the highest quality. If you have enjoyed this book, you will also like exploring our list of other titles.

Field Notes
DEER ISLAND *Neil Ansell*
ORISON FOR A CURLEW *Horatio Clare*
LOVE, MADNESS, FISHING *Dexter Petley*
WATER AND SKY *Neil Sentance*

Monographs
HERBACEOUS *Paul Evans*
ON SILBURY HILL *Adam Thorpe*
THE ASH TREE *Oliver Rackham*
MERMAIDS *Sophia Kingshill*
BLACK APPLES OF GOWER *Iain Sinclair*
BEYOND THE FELL WALL *Richard Skelton*
HAVERGEY *John Burnside*
SNOW *Marcus Sedgwick*

Nature Classics Library
THROUGH THE WOODS *H.E. Bates*
MEN AND THE FIELDS *Adrian Bell*
THE MIRROR OF THE SEA *Joseph Conrad*
ISLAND YEARS, ISLAND FARM *Frank Fraser Darling*
THE MAKING OF THE ENGLISH LANDSCAPE *W.G. Hoskins*
A SHEPHERD'S LIFE *W.H. Hudson*
BROTHER TO THE OX *Fred Kitchen*
FOUR HEDGES *Clare Leighton*
DREAM ISLAND *R.M. Lockley*
THE UNOFFICIAL COUNTRYSIDE *Richard Mabey*
RING OF BRIGHT WATER *Gavin Maxwell*
EARTH MEMORIES *Llewelyn Powys*
IN PURSUIT OF SPRING *Edward Thomas*
THE NATURAL HISTORY OF SELBORNE *Gilbert White*

A postcard sent to Little Toller will ensure you are put on our mailing list and amongst the first to discover each new book as it appears in the series. You can also follow our latest news at **littletoller.co.uk** or visit our online magazine **theclearingonline.org** for new essays, short films and poetry.

LITTLE TOLLER BOOKS
Lower Dairy, Toller Fratrum, Dorset DT2 0EL
W. littletoller.co.uk **E.** books@littletoller.co.uk